ANOTHER LOGIC WORKBOOK FOR GRITTY KIDS

created by Dan Allbaugh   illustrated by Anil Yap

Table of Contents

Hello there, my friend. You're here for book two.
There's fun to be had in these pages for you.
We're at it once more with a new set of tasks.
From fresh to familiar, each one is a blast!

Some of these puzzles are tricky, it's true,
but the harder the climb, the better the view.
If an answer's unclear, don't give up so quick,
pause and reflect and it may just click.

If you stare and you strain and you can't get results,
team up with a friend or a helpful adult.
The back has the answers! They'll show you the way.
They're there as a guide for the next time you play.

Most important of all, when it comes to success,
is knowing you tried and you gave it your best .

FIND THE HIDDEN MEEPLE

SOMEWHERE INSIDE!

Spatial Reasoning

Ready, set, go! You're about to dive in.
Fun spatial games are where we begin.
How does this fit? What's the location?
Take your mind for a spin to envision rotation.

If you try but fall short, don't scrap the whole lesson.
Keep poking and prodding, and ask some new questions!
The road to success might be lined with defeat,
but that road is a journey that you can complete.

Match the folded and cut paper with the unfolded paper shapes. Write your answers in the gray boxes.

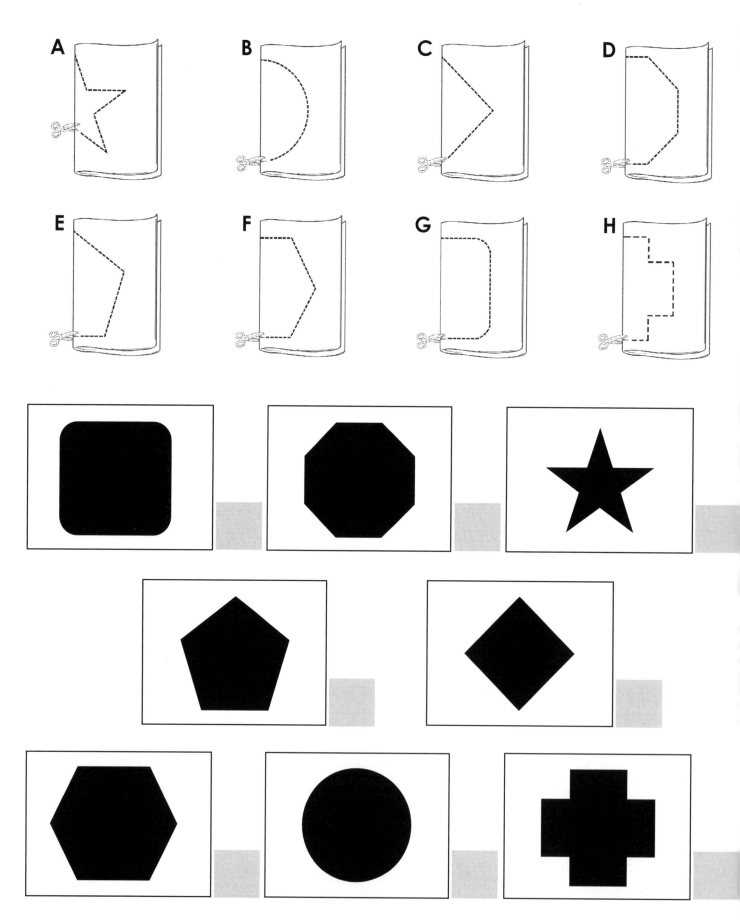

For each of the puzzles below, circle the piece which would best complete the missing square.

Bison got separated from her herd. Can you help her get back?

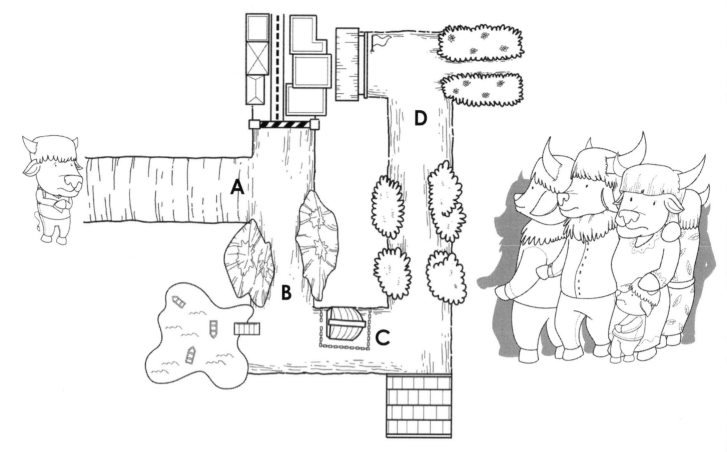

Using the landmarks on the map above,
can you help Bison decide which way to turn at each intersection?
Circle the correct answers.

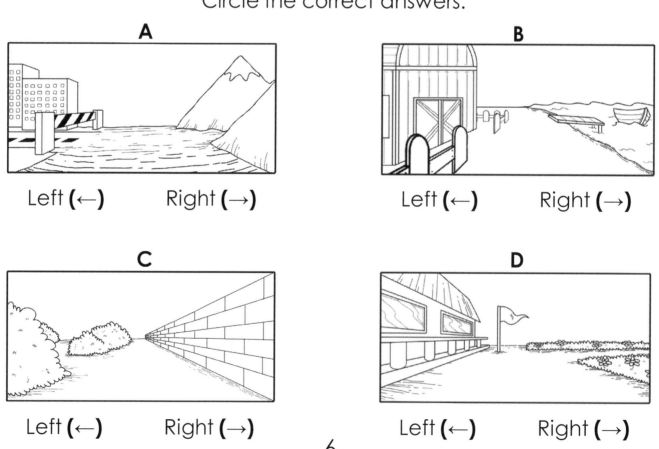

A

Left (←)   Right (→)

B

Left (←)   Right (→)

C

Left (←)   Right (→)

D

Left (←)   Right (→)

For each puzzle, connect the two black dots while drawing a continuous line that passes through every gray dot. The line can only go horizontally (↔) or vertically (↕).

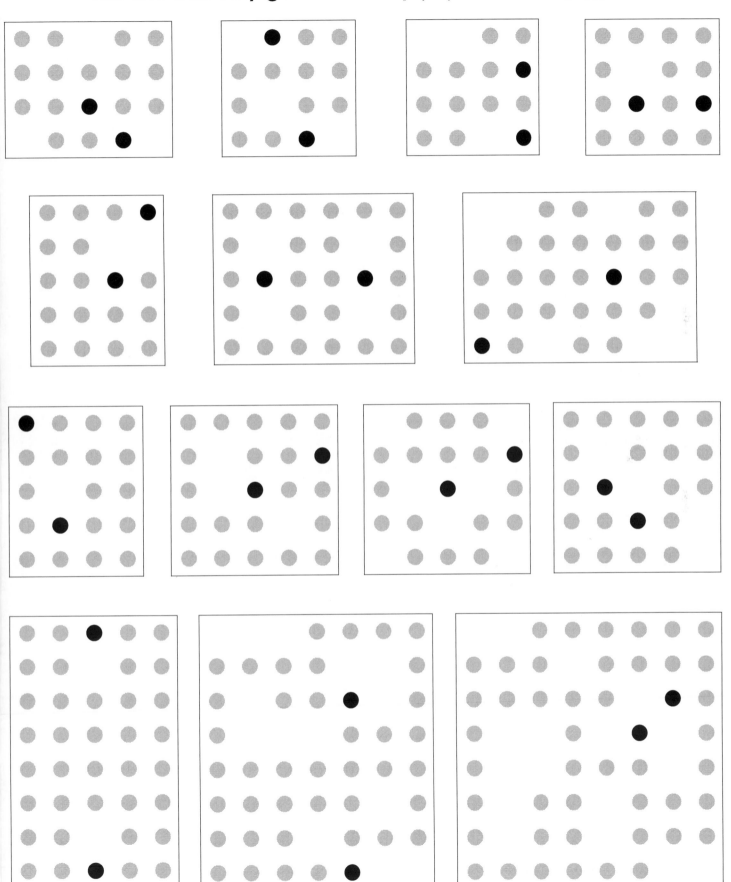

Draw a horizontal (↔) or vertical (↕) line to match one bird to one feather
Lines cannot cross over birds, feathers, or each other.
Connect all birds and feathers.

8

Can you complete the other half of these drawings?

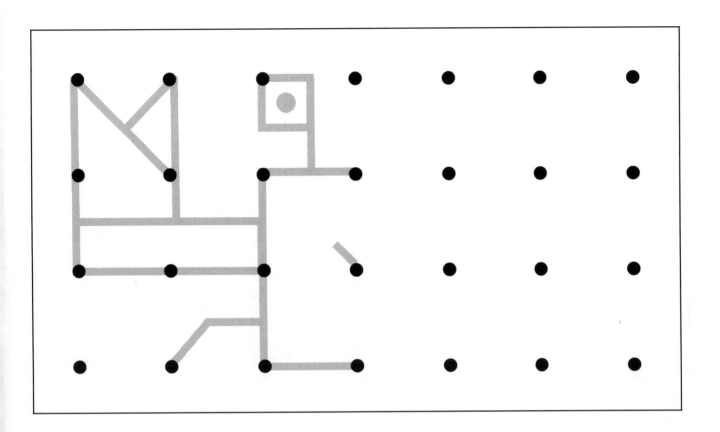

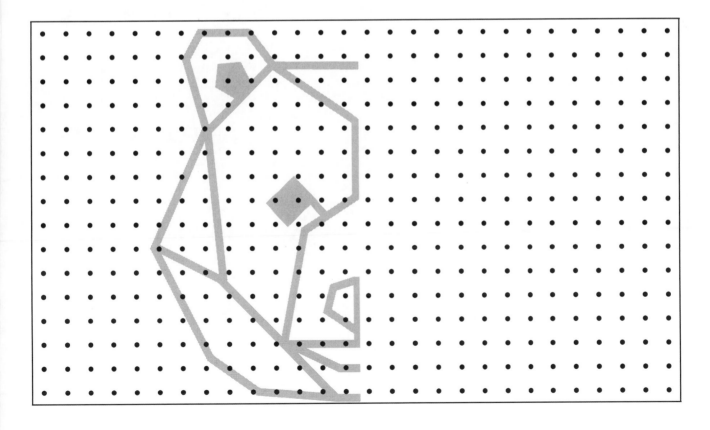

For each shape, make a continuous line that stays on the gray path and passes through all the dots. Begin on any dot you choose. No retracing over lines, but you may pass through dots more than once

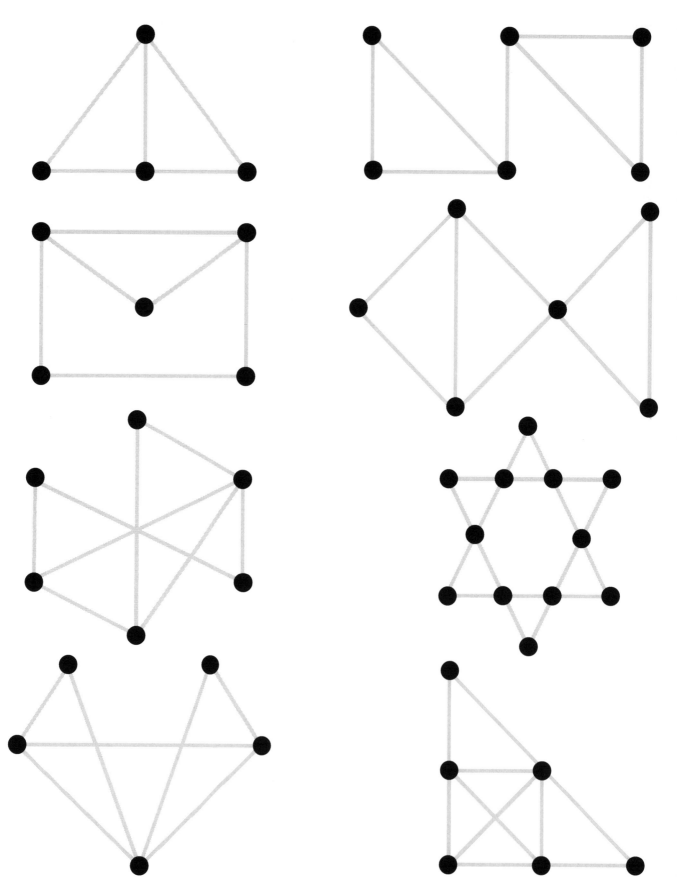

Each of these knots is different.
Count the number of ropes in each knot.

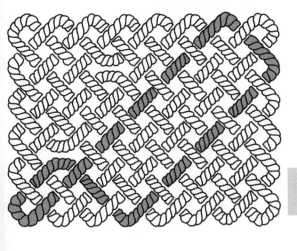

2

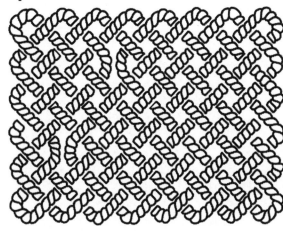

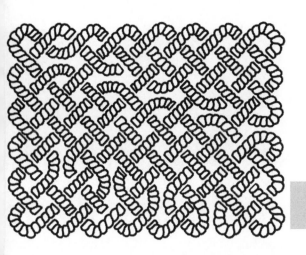

How many eggs are there?

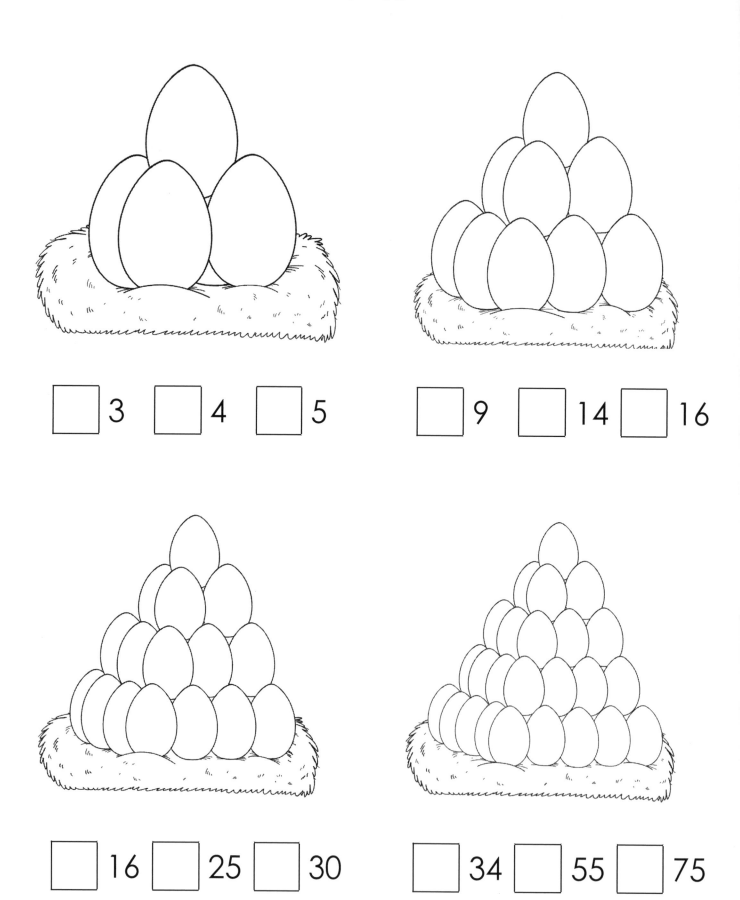

3   4   5

9   14   16

16   25   30

34   55   75

Which way will the gray gear spin? Circle the correct answer.

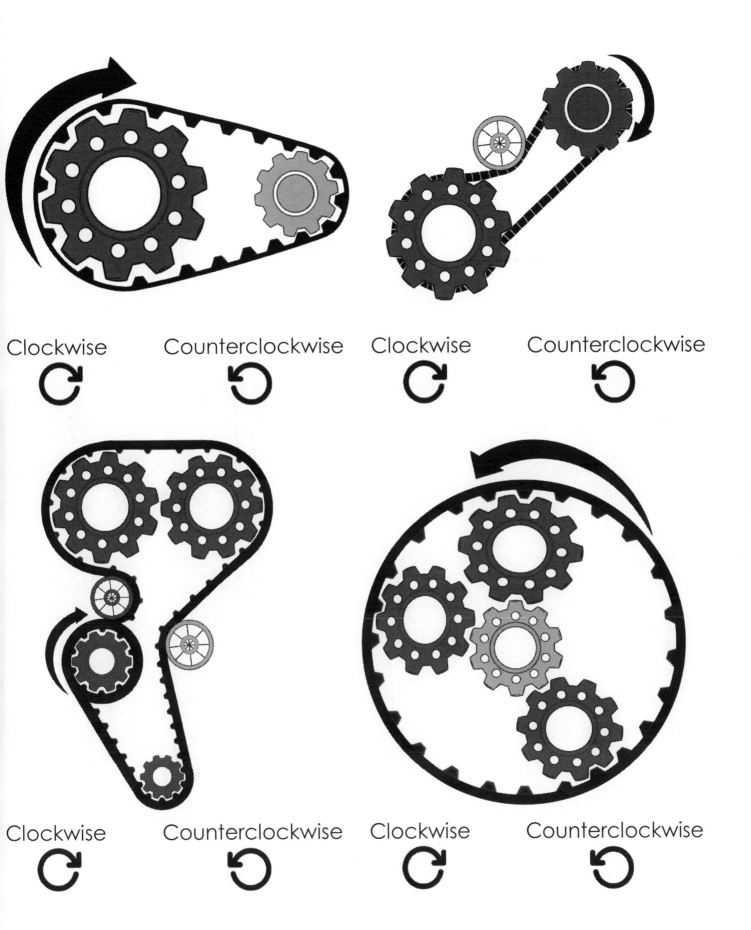

Clockwise   Counterclockwise   Clockwise   Counterclockwise

Clockwise   Counterclockwise   Clockwise   Counterclockwise

For each puzzle, connect the two black dots while drawing a continuous line that passes through every gray dot. The line can only go horizontally (↔) or vertically (↕).

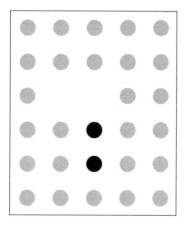

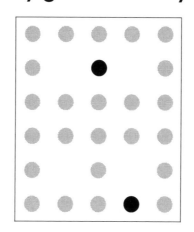

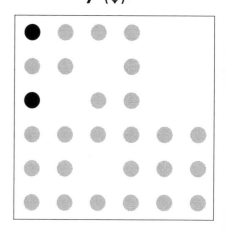

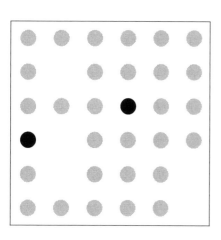

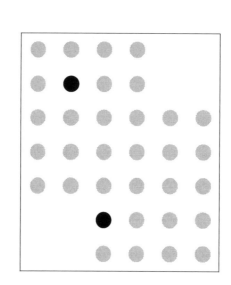

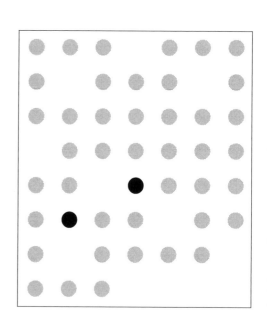

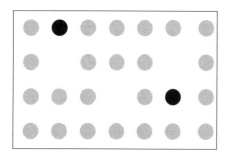

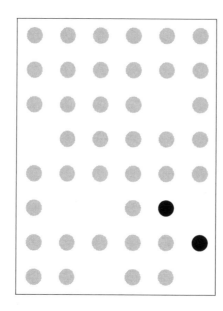

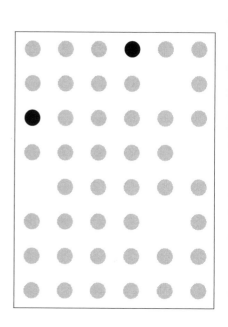

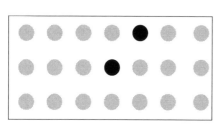

For each puzzle below, make three straight lines which create four animal groupings.

Each group should contain one of each of these animals:

Each group should contain one of each of these animals:

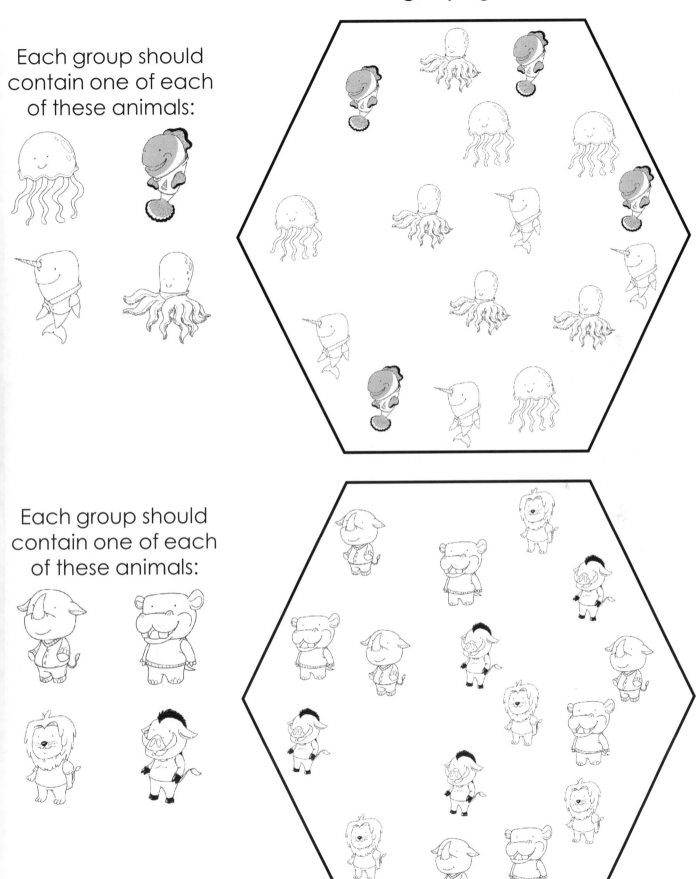

Circle the cube which cannot be made using each set of squares.

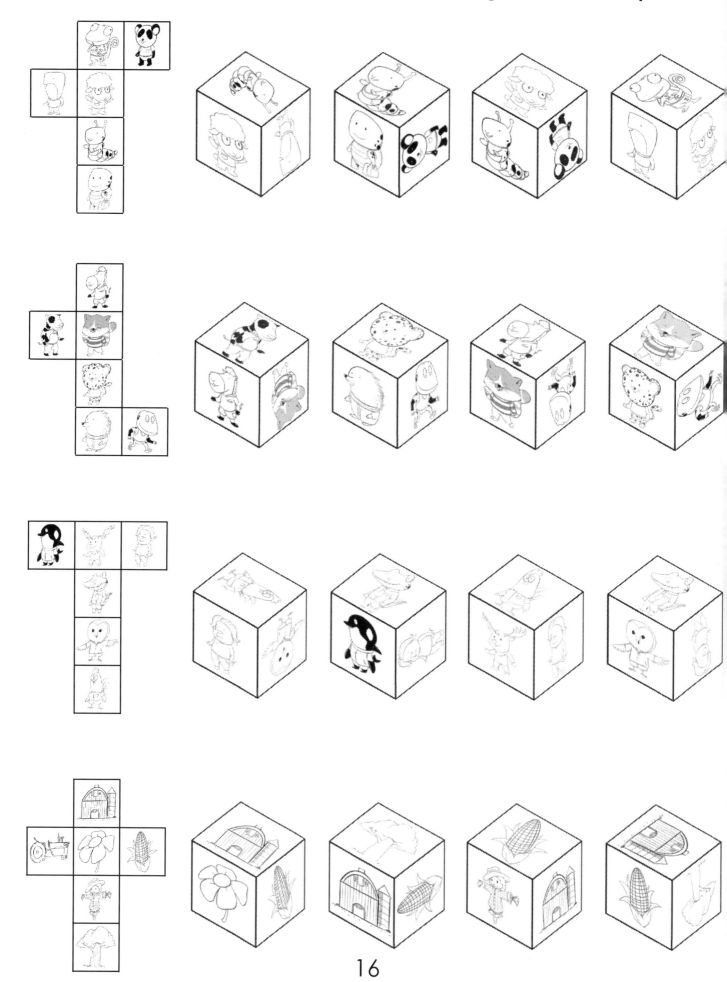

What formation in group 2 matches the identical but rotated formation in group 1?

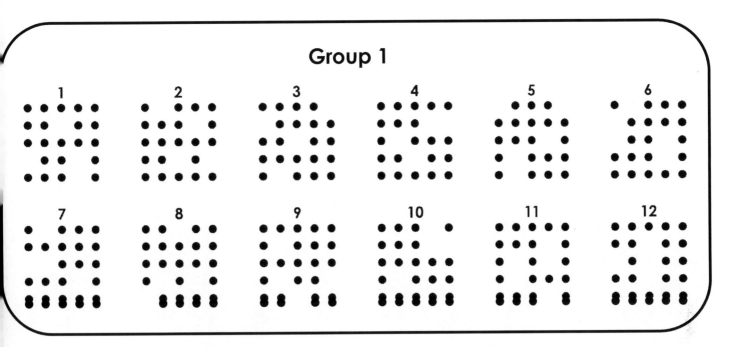

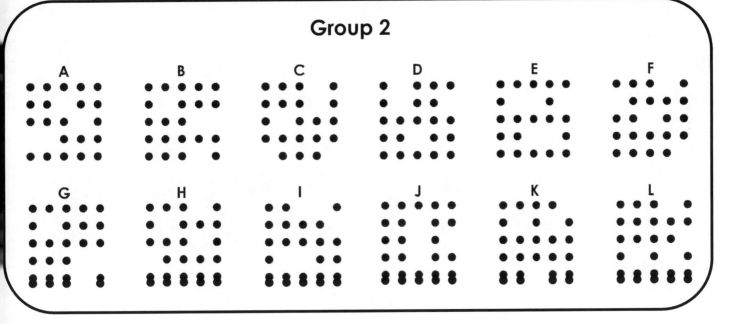

1 = ▢ 5 = ▢ 9 = ▢

2 = ▢ 6 = ▢ 10 = ▢

3 = ▢ 7 = ▢ 11 = ▢

4 = ▢ 8 = ▢ 12 = ▢

17

Connect each profile view to the group of blocks used to build it.

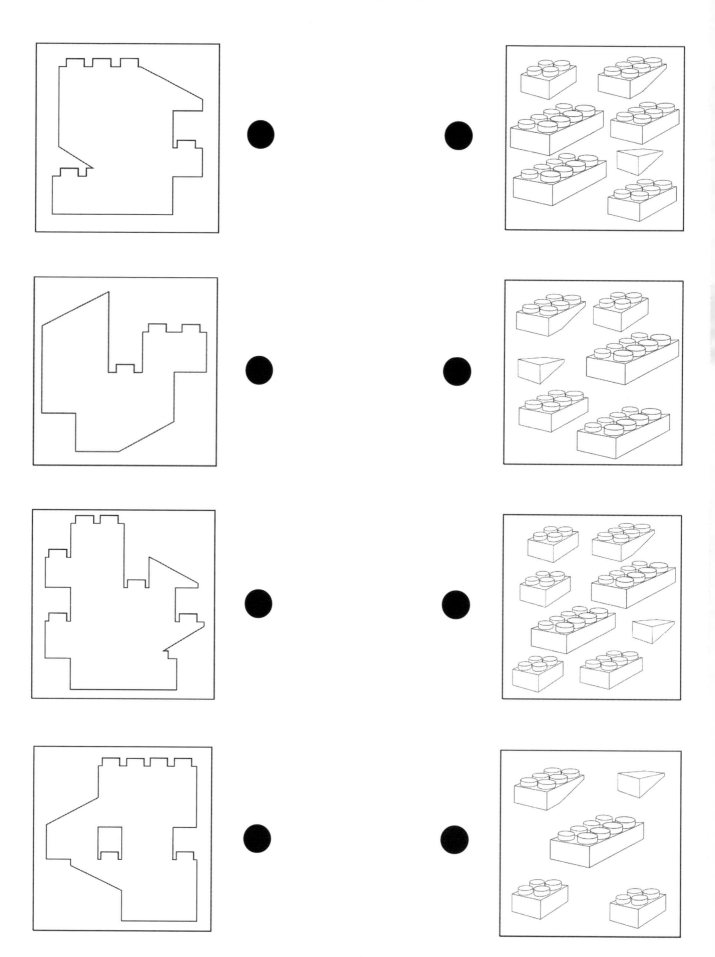

Use the following set of blocks to solve each puzzle.

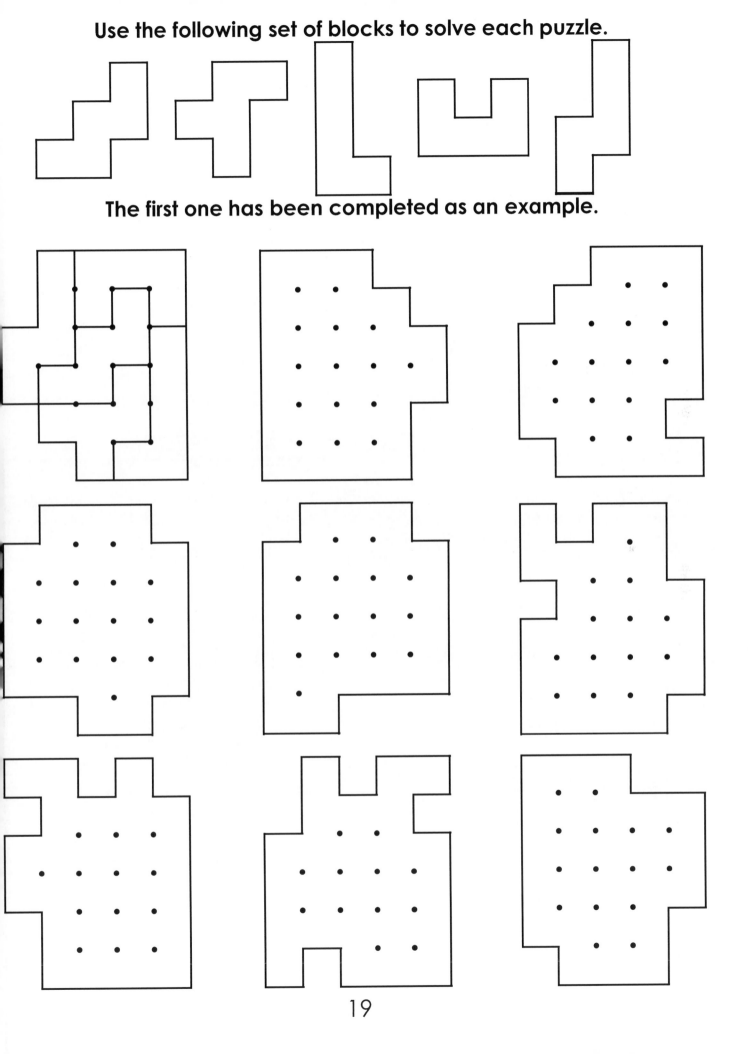

The first one has been completed as an example.

Fun with lines!
One of these is not possible. Can you figure out which one?

Draw four straight lines through the center of each dot to make a perfect square.

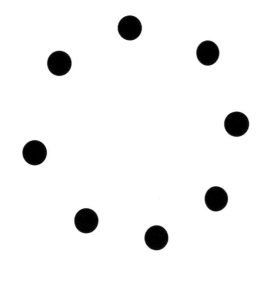

Connect the matching trees without crossing lines and staying inside the box.

Connect each of the three animals to each of the three clothing items using nine lines. Lines cannot cross animals, clothing, or each other.

Cut this treat into nine pieces using three straight lines. Pieces do not have to be equal sizes.

20

Math Puzzles

Arithmetic games are here in this lot.
Now roll up your sleeves. Give them all that you've got.
But attitude counts, so I have to insist
that when problems feel hard, you have grit and persist.

You're awesome. You're competent—totally capable.
Trust that your spirit is truly unbreakable.
Shoot for the stars. Aspire to be great.
Push boundaries with passion. Your triumph awaits!

Can you find the bush where Squirrel hid her acorns?
Begin at the star. Move around the map using the clues in order.

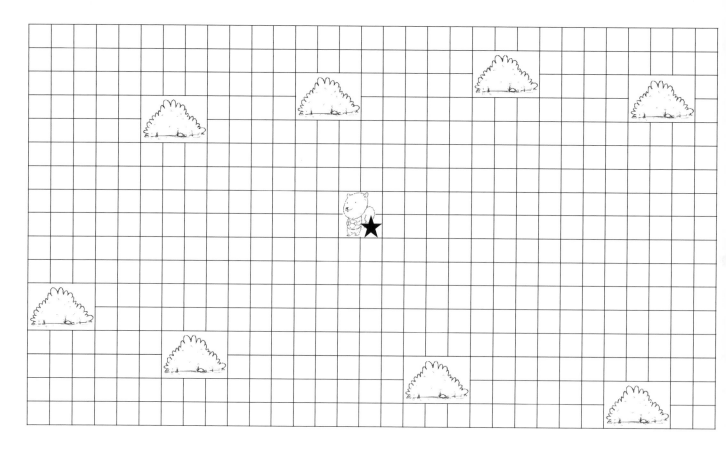

1. Go right (→) 3 + ___ = 15

2. Go down (↓) ___ + 7 = 13

3. Go left (←) ___ + 7 = 10

4. Go up (↑) 15 – 5 = ___

5. Go right (→) 15 - ___ = 9

6. Go down (↓) 12 - 4 = ___

7. Go left (←) 6 + 4 = ___

8. Go down (↓) ___ + 10 = 14

9. Go left (←) 5 + ___ = 12

10. Go up (↑) 8 + ___ = 19

11. Go right (→) 7 + ___ = 12

12. Go down (↓) 6 + ___ = 12

13. Go left (←) 16 – 8 = ___

14. Go up (↑) 19 - 10 = ___

15. Go left (←) ___ + 7 = 12

16. Go up (↑) 6 – 4 = ___

17. Go right (→) 13 - ___ = 10

18. Go down (↓) ___ + 6 = 15

19. Go left (←) 3 + ___ = 10

20. Go down (↓) 10 - 8 = ___

Spider caught lots of flies but can only eat three!
For each spiderweb, find the highest possible total value of flies.
Start anywhere and collect three flies by following the webbed path.
No jumping or going back over a path twice.

Lambie is looking for 24, his favorite number!
In each of the grids below there is only one time four numbers in a two-by-two square add up to 24. Can you find each of them?

4	1	6	8	4	4	6	1
1	1	2	6	2	1	4	6
5	4	1	7	1	4	3	6
2	6	7	6	6	8	6	7
4	1	1	8	4	7	6	3
2	9	5	2	4	2	5	6
1	8	9	3	8	5	9	7
2	6	5	1	7	8	9	7

5	8	4	6	6	1	1	1
7	9	2	8	3	8	4	3
1	4	1	6	5	2	6	9
8	9	7	1	4	8	9	1
5	2	7	4	8	8	1	4
5	5	3	2	7	2	2	9
4	2	1	2	8	9	4	2
4	7	1	9	2	2	5	4

2	8	9	4	3	8	6	7
1	1	5	6	5	6	3	9
6	5	7	8	9	3	7	4
5	9	9	9	5	8	2	5
7	8	2	3	3	6	3	5
1	9	6	1	9	9	8	2
7	4	3	1	5	6	7	9
7	3	1	9	1	1	8	1

4	5	2	1	4	1	6	1
5	4	9	4	4	5	7	1
5	3	6	1	9	2	8	1
9	1	4	1	5	2	6	5
6	2	5	1	5	9	1	2
3	2	2	5	7	1	6	8
2	2	2	2	9	8	5	5
5	5	5	8	2	1	9	7

Each block in a pyramid is the sum of the two numbers below it. Can you complete each pyramid?

Within every large square, each row (↔), column (↕), and mini-grid must contain the numbers 1, 2, 3, and 4.

		2	1
1			3
4			
		1	

	1		2
3		1	
		2	3

		3	
1			
2			3
	1	4	

	1	3	
3			
1	2		
			1

	4		
2			3
1			
	3	1	

2			
	1		2
		2	
4			1

Which animal is the heaviest? Which is the lightest?

Circle the heaviest. Put a square around the lightest.

**Fill in the gray squares with the correct number
to make each equation true.**

3	+		=		■		+	1	+	9	−	5	=	8
+	■	−	■	−	■	−	■	■	■	−	■	+	■	+
9	−	5	=	4	■	2	+	12	−	8	+		=	
+	■	+	■	−	■	=	■	−	■	+	■	−	■	−
8	−	4	=	4	■		−		+	7	−	4	=	0
−	■	−	■	=	■	■	■	−	■	+	■	−	■	−
	−	4	−		=		■	2	■		−		=	5
−	■	+	■	■	■	−	■	=	■	=	■	=	■	−
5	−		+	12	−	4	+		=		■	3	■	2
=	■	=	■	■	■	+	■	■	■	■	■	■	■	=
4	■	9	■	3	+	4	=		■	7	+		=	
■	■	■	■	+	■	+	■	−	■	■	■	−	■	■
10	−	2	−		=		■	2	+		+	6	=	9
+	■	+	■	−	■	+	■	+	■	+	■	−	■	+
	+		−	4	=	6	■		−	1	−	4	=	
−	■	−	■	+	■	=	■	=	■	+	■	+	■	−
	+	5	−	3	=		■	11	−	4	=	7	■	2
=	■	=	■	=	■	■	■	■	■	=	■	=	■	=
6	−		+	8	−		=	7	■	6	+		=	

Orangutan is looking for a specific number of bananas.
Find the path of numbers that add up to the sum at the exit arrow.
For each puzzle, start at the top left banana,
then step down (↓) or right (→) with each move.

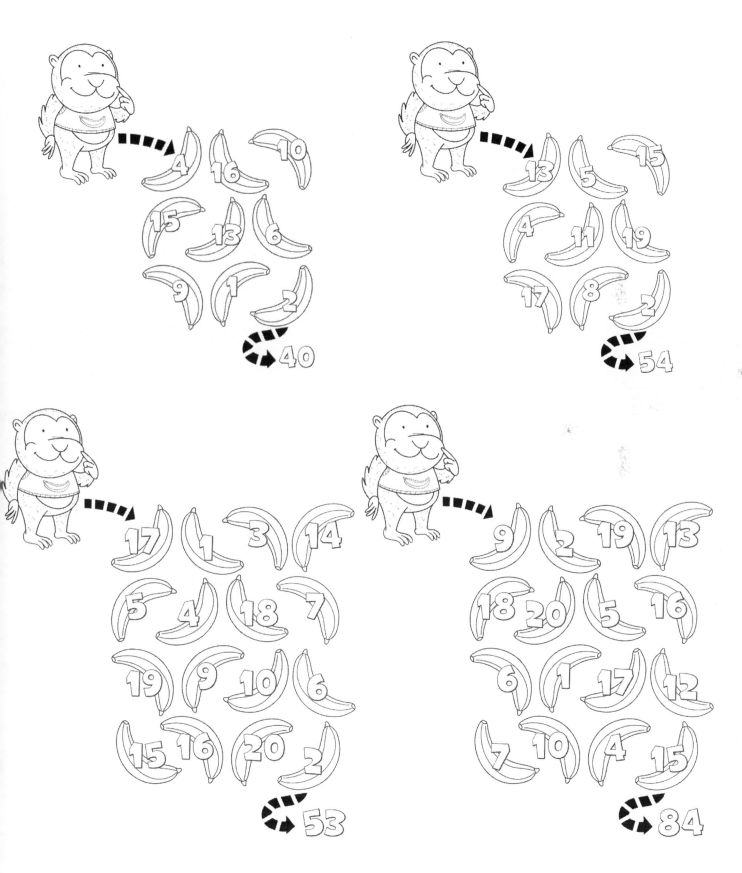

Within every large square, each row (↔), column (↕), and mini-grid must contain the numbers 1, 2, 3, 4, 5, and 6.

Puzzle 1 (top left):

		6	4	2	1
	4				6
1				3	4
	2				5
5		2	6		3
				1	2

Puzzle 2 (top right):

		5			
6				5	4
			2		
2		1	4	3	
5	4		1	2	3
1	2	3			6

Puzzle 3 (middle left):

5		3			
	4		5		3
				5	
4	6		3		2
		1		6	
6			2	3	

Puzzle 4 (middle right):

2					3
					5
		6			4
3				1	2
		5			

Puzzle 5 (bottom left):

			1		
	4				
3	2	4			
5					
	4	6	2		
		3			

Puzzle 6 (bottom right):

	6				
	3				5
	3		2		4
4	2			1	
	5				

Each puzzle must contain all numbers 1 to 9.
Some numbers have been provided.
Fill in the gray boxes to make the equations true.

Puzzle 1 (top left)

	+	6	+		= 18
-		+		+	
8	-		+	2	= 5
+		-		+	
	+	4	-		= 10
= 8		= 7		= 6	

Puzzle 2 (top right)

2	+		-		= 6
+		+		+	
	-	1	-		= 1
-		-		-	
3	+		-		= 0
= 6		= 3		= 0	

Puzzle 3 (middle left)

7	-		-		= 2
+		+		+	
2	+		-		= 6
-		-		-	
	-		+	6	= 11
= 1		= 10		= 0	

Puzzle 4 (middle right)

	+		+		= 24
+		+		+	
6	+		+		= 12
+		+		+	
	+		+	1	= 9
= 20		= 15		= 10	

Puzzle 5 (bottom left)

9	-		-		= 0
-		+		+	
	-	3	-		= 0
-		-		-	
	+		-	5	= 3
= 0		= 5		= 0	

Puzzle 6 (bottom right)

	+		+		= 15
+		+		+	
	+	5	+		= 15
+		+		+	
	+		+		= 15
= 15		= 15		= 15	

31

In this grid are hidden 63 addition and subtraction problems.
The equations may be positioned: ➡ ⬇ ⬊ ⬈
Can you find them all and complete the equation?
One is marked to help get you started. Not all numbers will be used.

10	20	4	9	12	10	5	15	5	17	9	2	4	4	8
2	10	9	5	10	9	6	7	2	5	12	1	7	8	5
12	10	13	4	2	3	10	12	5	7	9	5	17	1	6
4	5	9	12	9	5	8	11	4	7	8	9	6	8	7
1	3	6	5	9	6	1	8	7	4	8	16	14	8	7
10	6	8	1	13	2	7	17	9	7	7	3	11	6	4
6	7	15	6	6	10	7	11	16	4	13	13	7	2	3
4	12	1	6	5	19	3	6	14	3	3	9	4	2	5
3	10	6	2	10	6	9	1	3	6	3	14	4	6	12
11	7	5	4	2	9	9	10	6	15	8	8	2	14	2
10	4	7	3	12	8	12	4	9	8	9	4	7	6	10
2	3	9	10	2	5	9	5	5	7	15	7	7	10	3
8	4	16	1	3	7	6	17	7	7	6	9	5	10	6
11	3	8	2	1	5	1	4	3	10	9	4	2	20	9
3	3	6	6	7	5	12	10	12	6	6	13	9	9	18

The marked equation: $19 - 9 = 10$

Fill in each grid with numbers to make a connected path.
Count by a different number as shown above each grid.
You can connect numbers horizontally (↔) and vertically (↕).

Connect 1 to 36 counting by 1

		27	28		
	35				
23	36				10
22				8	9
				7	
		16	3		

Connect 2 to 72 counting by 2

		26	36		
	18			44	
14		30	32		48
12		8	6		50
	68			54	
		64	62		

Connect 3 to 108 counting by 3

9			36		42
			27		
			24	51	108
72	69	60			
		63			
78		84			99

Connect 4 to 144 counting by 4

140	144			84	80
136					76
			60	64	
			56	4	
124					24
120	116			32	28

Connect 5 to 180 counting by 5

		90			125
	50			115	
70			105		
		35			140
	15		150		
5			170		

Connect 6 to 216 counting by 6

102		90	36		24
	72			6	
	126			204	
144			156	174	186

Find your way down through this math maze.
You can only exit a cell if a number in the tunnel matches the answer.
Beware of dead ends!

Start

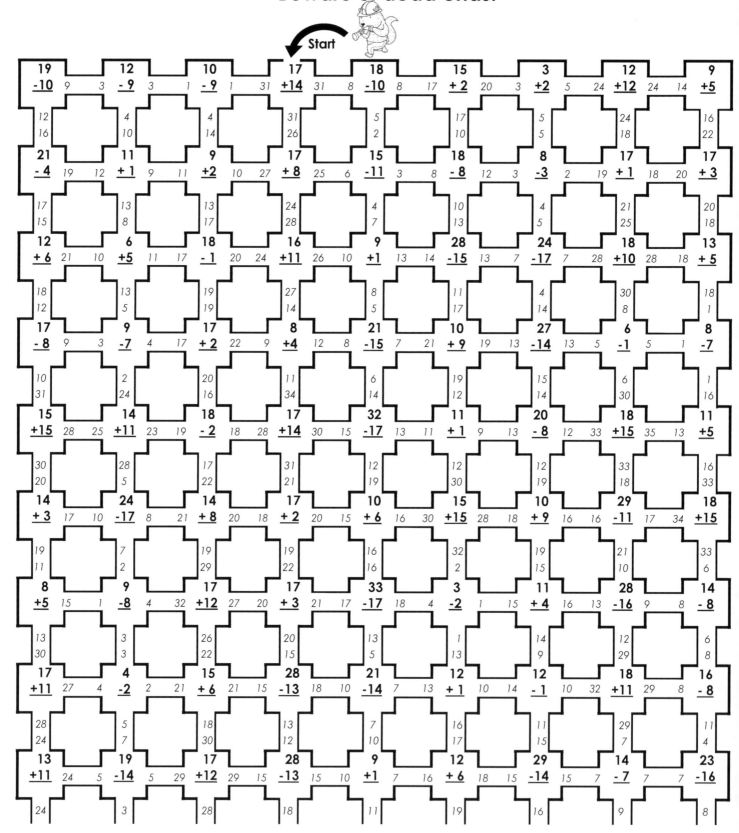

Finish

Each animal represents a number from 1 to 10. Use the equations to figure out each animal's number. Write your answers in the gray boxes.

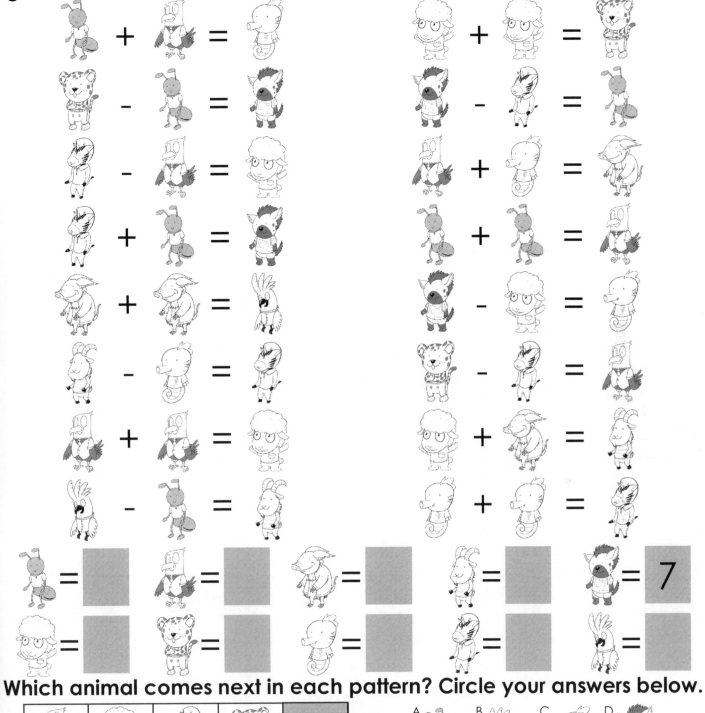

Which animal comes next in each pattern? Circle your answers below.

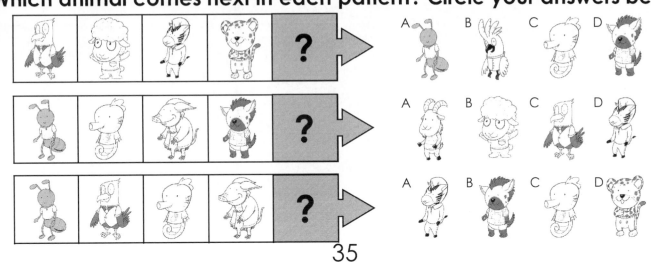

For each puzzle use all the available numbers one time. Your goal is to have the difference between connected circles all be unique numbers. The first one is completed as an example.

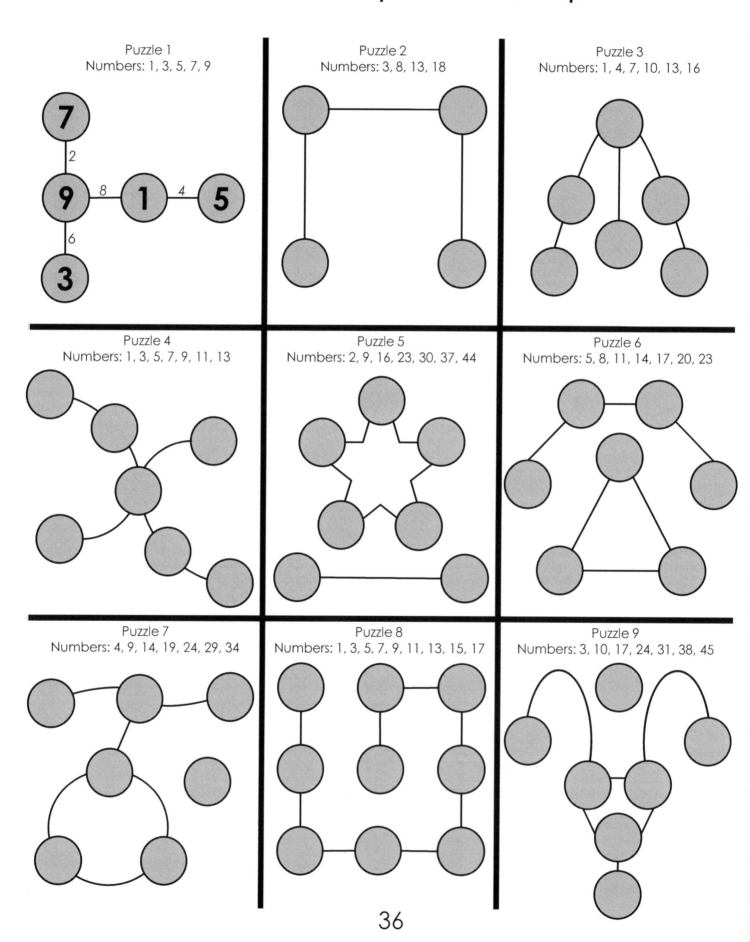

Puzzle 1
Numbers: 1, 3, 5, 7, 9

Puzzle 2
Numbers: 3, 8, 13, 18

Puzzle 3
Numbers: 1, 4, 7, 10, 13, 16

Puzzle 4
Numbers: 1, 3, 5, 7, 9, 11, 13

Puzzle 5
Numbers: 2, 9, 16, 23, 30, 37, 44

Puzzle 6
Numbers: 5, 8, 11, 14, 17, 20, 23

Puzzle 7
Numbers: 4, 9, 14, 19, 24, 29, 34

Puzzle 8
Numbers: 1, 3, 5, 7, 9, 11, 13, 15, 17

Puzzle 9
Numbers: 3, 10, 17, 24, 31, 38, 45

Logic Problems

Imagine big things! Dream wide awake!
Have goals for yourself and the life that you make!
Don't ever give up. That's easy to do.
Be gritty. Be strong. Be the very best you.

It's important to try, and it's OK to fail.
You'll keep making progress and one day prevail.
The following games will challenge your mind.
I know you can do this. It's time that you shined.

In each section, circle the animals that meet the conditions indicated.

Animals which eat plants and are mammals.

| LOBSTER | FROG | PARAKEET | WOLF | KOALA |

Animals which have a pattern or swim.

| EARTHWORM | DOLPHIN | COW | SCORPION | ORCA |

Animals which do not lay eggs.

| OTTER | CROCODILE | TORTOISE | PIG | DUCK |

Animals which are birds and can fly, or animals which are extinct.

| OSTRICH | TRICERITOPS | HORSE | ROOSTER | PENGUIN |

Every day one animal is the leader and chooses the group play activity.
Which animal is the group leader each day?

- Tortoise leads on a weekend day.
- Orangutan leads four days before Tiger.
- Camel leads between Lambie and Sloth.
- Tiger gets to lead on Fridays.
- Sloth and Lambie are leaders two days apart.
- Warthog is the leader three days after Camel.
- Lambie is the leader the day after Orangutan.

Can you draw lines to connect each animal to the day they are the leader?

Sunday	Monday	Tuesday	Wednesday	Thursday	Friday	Saturday
●	●	●	●	●	●	●

WARTHOG   TIGER   LAMBIE   SLOTH

CAMEL   ORANGUTAN   TORTOISE

Where is Tiger hiding?

Using the map and clues provided below, circle the only spot on the map where Tiger could be hiding.

Clues:

- Tiger is hiding within one space of water.
- Tiger is not hiding within one space of a desert.
- Tiger is hiding within one space of a mountain.
- Tiger is not hiding within one space of a forest.
- Tiger is hiding in the grasslands.

water desert mountain forest grasslands

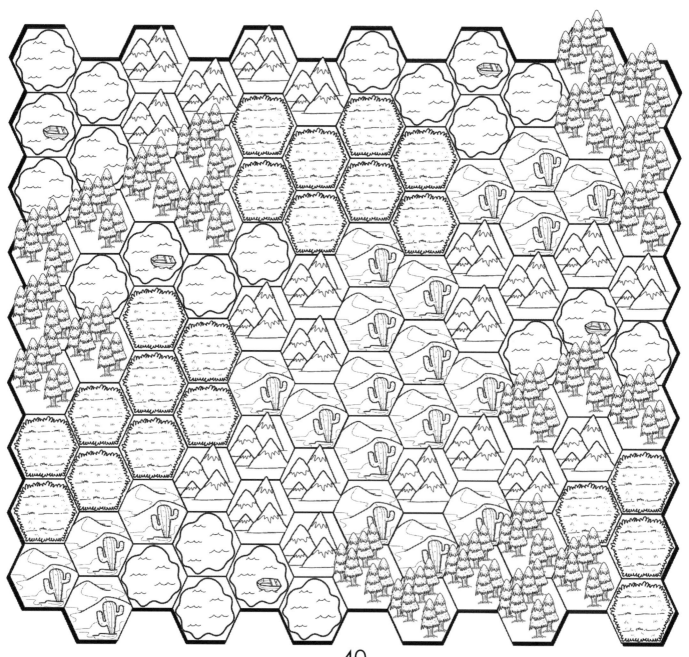

40

Can you connect each animal to their location?

- Peacock isn't in a corner, but Spider is.
- Leopard is the farthest distance from Giraffe, who is next to Turkey.
- Seal is in the same column (↕) as Mouse, who is in the same row (↔) as Fox.

Fill in each grid so that each column (↕) and row (↔) contains the numbers 1, 2, 3, and 4.
Boxes connected by a line mean the numbers are consecutive.
The absence of a line means numbers are not consecutive.

Puzzle 1

Puzzle 2

Puzzle 3

Puzzle 4

Fill in each grid so that each column (↕) and row (↔) contains the numbers 1, 2, 3, and 4.
Pairs of numbers must satisfy the inequality signs of greater than (>) and less than (<).

Puzzle 1

Puzzle 2

Puzzle 3

Puzzle 4

What day is it today?

- Piano lessons start in the prior week before the tennis tournament.
- There is no chess club today.
- Today is not an even day.
- Alpaca's tennis tournament is the last Saturday of the month.
- Today is a school day.
- Alpaca starts taking piano lessons in two weeks.
- Alpaca has chess club on Thursdays.

Can you use this calendar to figure out today's date?

Sunday	Monday	Tuesday	Wednesday	Thursday	Friday	Saturday
1	2	3	4	5	6	7
8	9	10	11	12	13	14
15	16	17	18	19	20	21
22	23	24	25	26	27	28
29	30	31				

Can you connect each animal to their location?

- Giraffe, Turkey, and Mouse are in the same row (↔).
- Lambie and Peacock are in opposite corners.
- Turkey, Giraffe, and Owl are next to Elephant.
- Peacock is next to Mouse.
- Fox and Seal are in the same row (↔).
- Lambie, Giraffe, and Spider are in the same column (↕).

Where does each animal live?

- Squirrel lives West of Lambie.
- Goat is neighbors with Skunk and Lambie.
- Raccoon lives in the Southeast.
- Horse lives in the Southern row.
- Cow lives directly East of Goat.
- Cat lives North of Raccoon and East of Lambie.
- Skunk lives East of Horse.
- Lambie lives in the Northern row.
- Pig lives South of Squirrel and West of Goat.

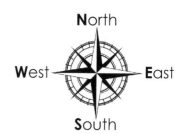

Can you draw a line from each animal to their house?

HORSE   CAT   RACCOON   COW   SKUNK   PIG   SQUIRREL   LAMBIE   GOAT

Where did Dog bury the bone?

Dog buried a bone somewhere on the island.
He gives you the following clues:

- It is not within two spaces of a hut.
- It is not in or next to a beach.
- It is within two spaces of a palm tree.

- It is next to, but not in a lake.
- It is next to a mountain.
- It is not next to the ocean.

- jungle
- mountain
- lake
- scrubland
- beach
- river
- palm tree
- hut
- ocean

Can you use those clues to figure out where the bone is buried?
Circle the correct hexagon below.

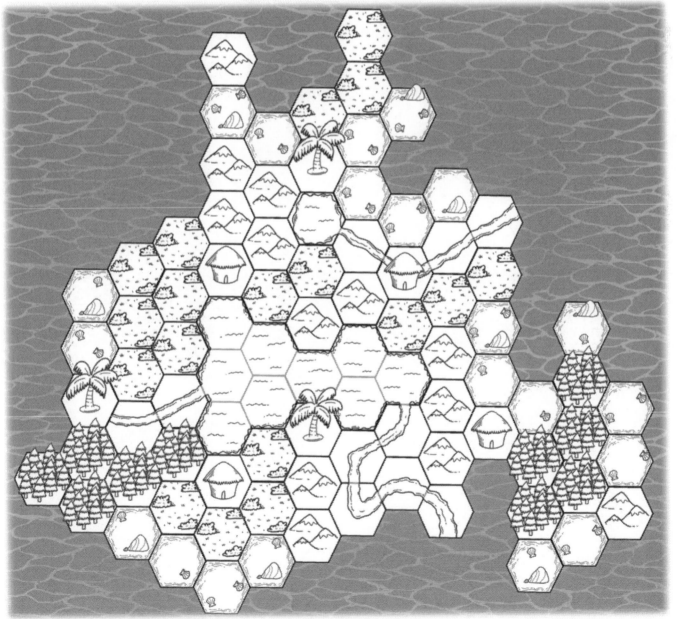

47

Connect the dots. Numbers show how many lines touch that dot. Draw lines horizontally (↔) or vertically (↕) only. There are two lines at most per dot. The first one is completed as an example.

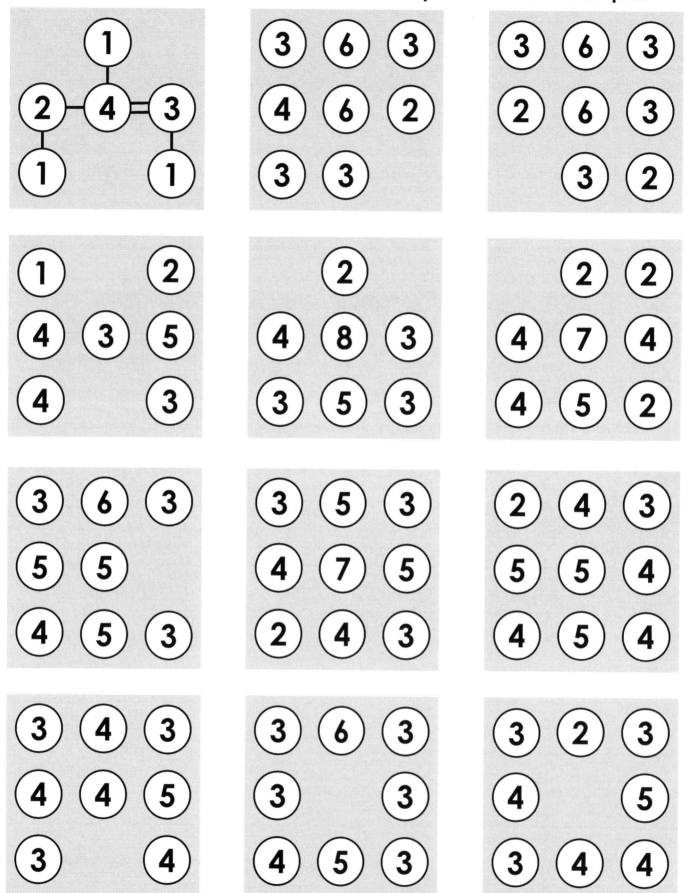

48

Can you connect each animal to their location?

- Toad and Leopard are in the same column (↕).
- Mouse is between Seal and Giraffe.
- Lambie and Leopard are as far apart as they can be.
- Turkey is in the same column (↕) as Peacock, who is in the same row (↔) as Elephant, who is in the same column (↕) as Spider, who is in the same row (↔) as Leopard.
- Fox is next to Giraffe.
- Mouse and Spider are in the same column (↕).

Twelve animals have birthdays in twelve different months. Which animal was born in which month?

- Lambie was born in a month which has a leap day.
- Rhinoceros has a birthday between Otter and Elephant.
- Walrus has more animals celebrating birthdays after her each year than before.
- Sloth's birthday is surrounded by Eagle and Mole.
- Eagle will have a birthday before Otter each year.
- Lion has a birthday three months before Squid.
- Polar Bear was born in the last month of the year.
- Mole will celebrate his birthday five months after Crab.
- Crab has the next birthday after Lambie.
- Otter has fewer people celebrating birthdays after him each year than before.
- Squid has a birthday eight months before Polar Bear.
- Elephant's birthday celebration is ten months after Lion's.

Can you draw lines to connect each animal to the month they were born in?

LAMBIE

WALRUS

MOLE

SLOTH

ELEPHANT

January	February	March
April	May	June
July	August	September
October	November	December

LION

EAGLE

RHINOCEROS

POLAR BEAR

CRAB

SQUID

OTTER

Fill in each grid so that each column (↕) and row (↔) contains the numbers 1, 2, 3, 4, and 5. Boxes connected by a line mean the numbers are consecutive. The absence of a line means numbers are not consecutive.

Puzzle 1

Puzzle 2

Puzzle 3

Puzzle 4

Fill in each grid so that each column (↕) and row (↔) contains the numbers 1, 2, 3, 4, and 5.
Pairs of numbers must satisfy the inequality signs of greater than (>) and less than (<).

Puzzle 1

1	4			3
			5	
2	^ 1			^
	<	<	< 4	
	> 4	>	< 2	

Puzzle 2

		1		4
2	^ >		^	1
		^	v	<
1	4	2		3
	3			

Puzzle 3

	2	5	1	
		2	3	1
	^ > 3		2	
			^	
				2

Puzzle 4

3	1			
	3			^
			4	^
1	2	3		^

52

Can you connect each animal to their location?

- Leopard is next to Lambie, Giraffe, and Seal.
- Peacock is next to Spider and Owl.
- Fox is next to Mouse.
- Toad is next to Peacock, Turkey, Giraffe, and Mouse.
- Mouse is next to Toad, Elephant, and Owl.
- Spider is in the same row (↔) as Turkey and Lambie.
- One of the clues above is wrong.

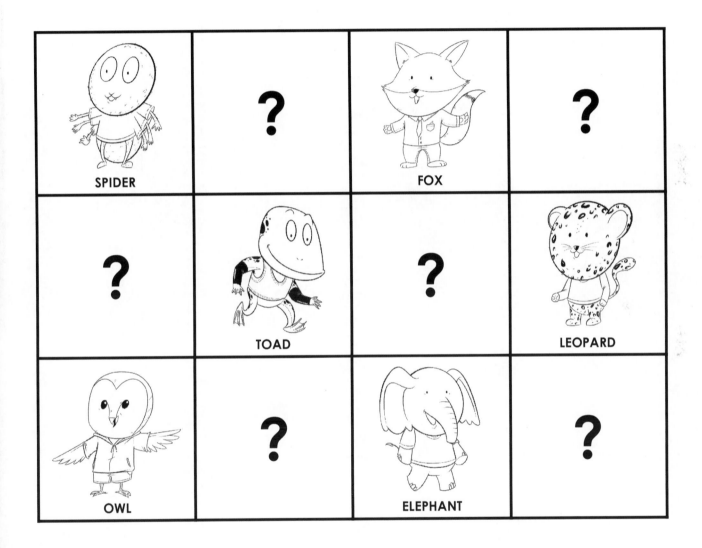

Connect the matching shapes without overlapping any lines or shapes

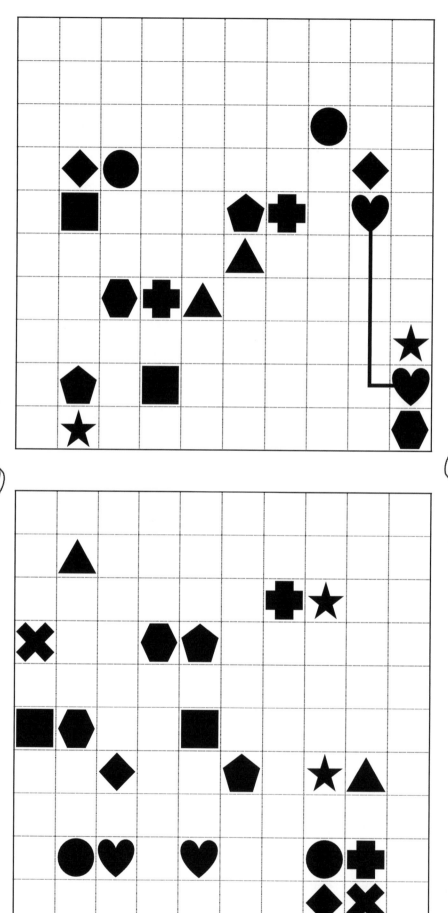

How long was everyone in the pool?

- Pool hours are 10:00am to 5:00pm.
- Alligator got in the pool when it opened and stayed in until noon.
- Beaver swam from 11:00am to 1:30pm with a 45-minute lunch break.
- Crab got in 15 minutes after Beaver and got out 30 minutes after Duck.
- Duck was in the pool twice as long as Alligator, and got out an hour before it closed.
- Lambie started swimming with Duck and got out with Salamander, but took three 15-minute breaks.
- Salamander swam for 30 minutes less than the next lowest animal and got out at 2:15pm.
- Platypus was at the pool from open until close, but only spent half her time swimming.
- Hippo started swimming with Salamander and got out an hour before Crab.

Can you fill out the gray boxes to show how long everybody spent in the pool and then order them from lowest total pool time to highest?

	Total Pool Time	Order		Total Pool Time	Order
Alligator	hours / minutes		**Lambie**	hours / minutes	
Beaver	hours / minutes		**Salamander**	hours / minutes	
Crab	hours / minutes		**Platypus**	hours / minutes	
Duck	hours / minutes		**Hippo**	hours / minutes	

Who ate the last piece of cake?

Lambie was saving the last piece of cake for dessert tonight, but he just discovered it had been eaten! He asks his friends about it.

- Meerkat says, "Vulture ate it!"
- Camel says, "Meerkat is telling the truth!"
- Gorilla says, "If Meerkat is lying, Camel is lying."
- Vulture says, "It wasn't Camel."
- Platypus saw the whole thing and says, "Only one of those animals is telling the truth."

Can you help Lambie use the clues to figure out who ate the last piece of cake? Write your answer in the gray box below.

ate the last piece of cake.

What is the three-digit combination for Lambie's bike lock?
Use these clues to help to figure it out.

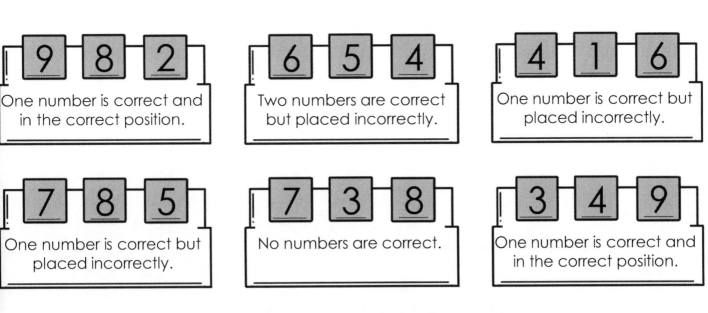

9 8 2 — One number is correct and in the correct position.

6 5 4 — Two numbers are correct but placed incorrectly.

4 1 6 — One number is correct but placed incorrectly.

7 8 5 — One number is correct but placed incorrectly.

7 3 8 — No numbers are correct.

3 4 9 — One number is correct and in the correct position.

What is the combination?

57

There is a race to the trophy! Each bird starts at the same time. When they reach a shape, they fly the represented steps.

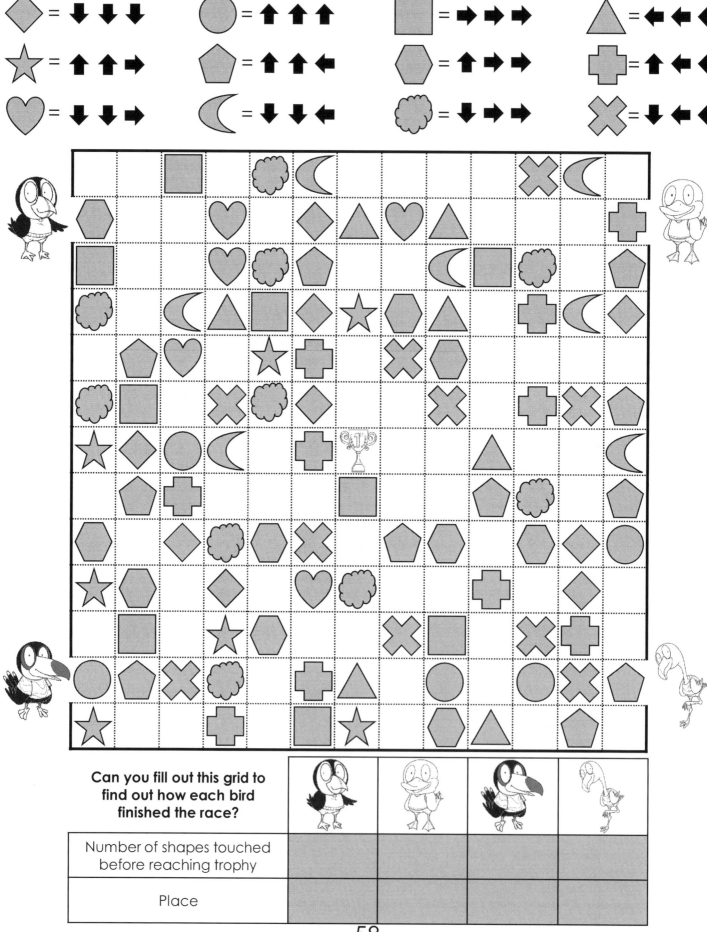

Can you fill out this grid to find out how each bird finished the race?				
Number of shapes touched before reaching trophy				
Place				

Can you solve these brainteasers?
The answer may not be so obvious.

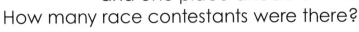

In a race, Chipmunk finished two places in front of last place and one place ahead of fifth.
How many race contestants were there?

If Cobra tells you, "Everything I say is a lie", is he telling the truth or a lie?

There are two snails in front of a snail, two snails behind a snail, and a snail in the middle. Those are all the snails. How many are there?

The day before two days after the day before tomorrow is Saturday.
What day is it today?

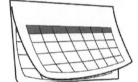

There are two ducks in front of two other ducks.
There are two ducks behind two other ducks.
There are two ducks beside two other ducks.
What is the minimum number of ducks there could be?

Add me to myself and multiply by four.
Divide me by eight, and you will have me once more.
What number am I?

Any daughter of Mama Bunny has as many sisters as brothers.
Each of her brothers has twice as many sisters as brothers.
How many sons does Mama Bunny have?
How many daughters?

Draw a single non-intersecting line between dots to form a loop.
Numbers specify how many sides touch the loop. The first one is started

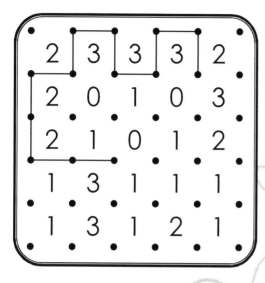

2	3	3	3	2
2	0	1	0	3
2	1	0	1	2
1	3	1	1	1
1	3	1	2	1

2	3	2	3	2
3	1	2	1	2
3	2	3	1	1
3	1	1	1	2
1	2	3	2	1

1	2	2	1	2	2
3	1	0	1	1	3
2	1	1	3	2	1
2	1	0	2	3	1
3	1	1	3	2	0
1	2	2	2	3	1

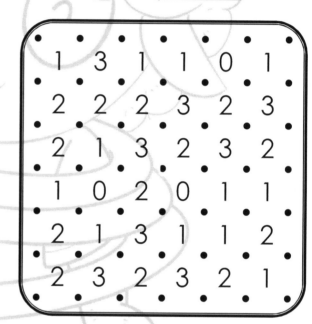

1	3	1	1	0	1
2	2	2	3	2	3
2	1	3	2	3	2
1	0	2	0	1	1
2	1	3	1	1	2
2	3	2	3	2	1

2	3	2	0	1	3	2
3	1	2	2	2	1	2
1	3	1	1	1	0	1
1	3	1	0	1	1	1
1	2	3	2	3	2	3
3	1	2	1	2	2	1
2	3	2	2	2	3	1

2	2	1	2	2	3	1
3	1	1	2	2	2	0
1	2	2	3	2	3	1
1	2	1	2	1	3	0
3	2	1	3	1	2	2
1	3	2	2	2	1	3
1	3	2	1	1	1	1

60

Can you connect each animal to their location?

- Mouse is next to (4) and (7). Lambie is next to (6) and (8).
- The right-most column (↕) adds up to (16).
- The top-most row (↔) adds up to (19).
- All animals in the middle row (↔) are more than (5).
- Leopard is next to Giraffe and Fox.

MOUSE	SEAL	?	?
GIRAFFE	?	?	TURKEY
?	?	ELEPHANT	LAMBIE

LEOPARD   TOAD   PEACOCK   SPIDER   FOX   OWL

Can you find all 10 snakes in the grass? Some are partially showing. Snakes can be (↔) or (↕) but don't intersect or share borders. The numbers indicate how many spaces in that row (↔) or column (↕) contain part of the snake. Mark all spots containing parts of a snake.

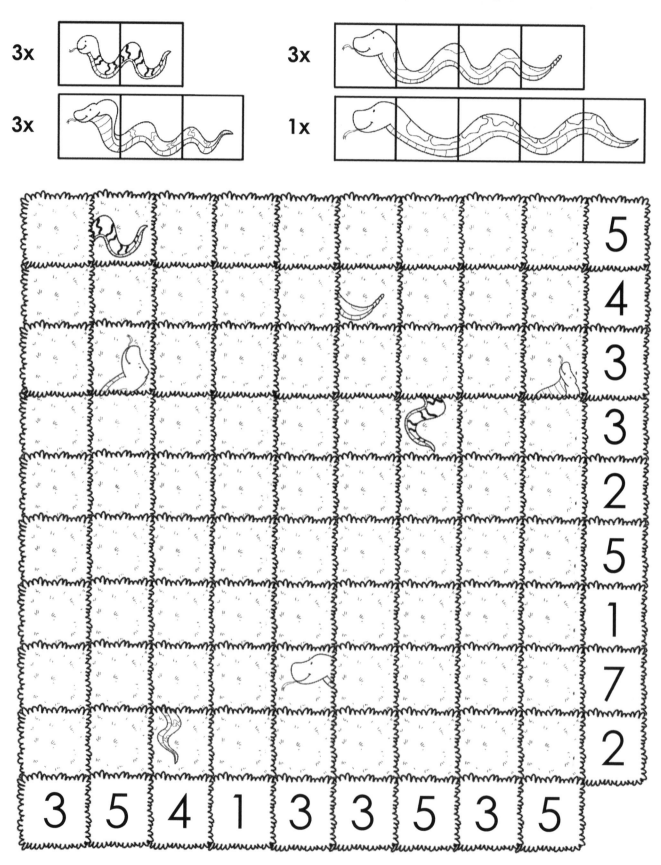

62

Word Games

Without any challenge, you won't see a change.
These puzzles are tough, but they're good for your brain.
You might mess it up, and you might answer wrong—
that feeling's not great, but it won't last for long.

Nobody counts your amount of mistakes.
Don't be hard on yourself. Give *you* a break.
The next focus here is on letters and words,
so turn the page over and steady your nerves.

Starting with the gray 'A', create a connected path that goes through the alphabet twice in order. You can connect letters horizontally (↔) and vertically (↕).

A	K	D	E	I	W	L	Z	Y	X
B	C	K	V	G	K	C	L	R	W
H	D	M	Y	M	N	O	H	U	V
G	E	G	N	L	C	P	G	T	G
U	F	U	J	K	T	Q	F	S	R
U	G	H	I	D	S	R	T	E	Q
E	Z	Y	X	W	T	O	D	O	P
T	A	D	E	V	U	L	M	N	A
V	B	C	F	I	J	K	T	E	R
E	Z	B	G	H	V	K	S	G	T

64

Sneaky Seagull is hungry and has stolen some food letters!
Match each group of food words to the nest with the missing letter.

C _ L _ R Y
W A T _ R M _ L O N
L _ M O N

P _ T A T _
C H _ C _ L A T E
C _ C _ N U T

_ O R N
_ A N D Y
T A _ O

K _ W _
C H _ P S
R _ C E

B _ R G E R
Y O G _ R T
S O _ P

B _ N N _ N _
_ V O C _ D O
G R _ N O L _

O R A _ G E
H O _ E Y
_ O O D L E

G _ A P E S
P E A _
_ A D I S H

Trace the lines to find out which box contains each letter to reveal a secret message.

Color in every C, G, J, K, Q, and X.
The remaining letters show a hidden message.

I C F Y O Q U F E G
E L J O V E C J R W
H E G K L M Q E D O
X N A P X U Z C Z L
E Y O J U C S T A Q
R T R E G M E M B X
E R T H K E S T C A
R T I J S Q T H K E
H A X R D G E S J T
O Q F G P A K R T S

Write the message below:

__ ___ ____ _____ __ _ _____ ___ _____'
_____ ___ _____ __ ___ _____ __ _____.

67

Change one letter at a time moving from the top to bottom word. Use the clues to help along your way.

HOT
- small spot
- move earth
- it barks

PIG

COW
- cut grass
- gives directions
- cleans floors

NAP

FOX
- repair broken
- be seated
- house animal
- a number
- small hole

PEN

BUG
- very large
- large pig
- body part
- muddy ground
- cut tree

LET

SAIL
- remove water
- ring this
- lightning strike
- round toy
- wear it

BOAT

DISH
- swimming animal
- high speed
- object price
- balled hand
- protective shell

COAT

Find the hidden words.
Words can go in these directions: → ← ↑ ↓ ↘ ↙ ↖ ↗

```
N  P  T  E  R  R  I  F  I  C  T  K  C  C  F
E  Z  E  E  O  B  G  W  R  G  S  H  Y  I  R
M  S  P  E  C  T  A  C  U  L  A  R  Y  T  I
O  U  E  S  S  X  T  H  H  U  A  L  R  S  A
S  V  X  I  I  U  J  P  Z  N  I  E  G  A  Y
E  K  C  L  W  W  O  Q  I  T  M  R  A  T  M
W  A  E  U  B  H  O  D  O  E  M  N  S  N  A
A  H  L  G  V  K  R  N  N  J  D  N  A  R
O  R  L  A  R  O  U  D  D  E  J  H  D  F  V
V  X  E  A  A  E  O  S  R  E  P  K  K  G  E
U  Q  N  R  O  U  A  M  N  G  R  U  E  D  L
L  O  T  G  S  D  Z  T  L  W  X  F  T  I  O
D  X  D  A  O  D  F  A  B  U  L  O  U  S  U
E  L  B  I  D  E  R  C  N  I  I  A  Z  L  S
I  A  S  Z  N  A  M  A  Z  I  N  G  E  A  G
```

AMAZING	EXTRAORDINARY	GREAT	SPECTACULAR	TERRIFIC
AWESOME	FABULOUS	INCREDIBLE	STUPENDOUS	TREMENDOUS
EXCELLENT	FANTASTIC	MARVELOUS	SUPER	WONDERFUL

Find the nine-letter animal names in each of these boxes. Start at the gray box and connect to the next box horizontally (↔), vertically (↕), or diagonally (⊠).

Y	L	R
F	D	A
N	O	G

T	E	A
H	R	R
W	O	M

I	O	W
N	R	L
E	E	V

E	I	P
N	O	U
P	R	C

K	O	O
C	D	W
U	H	C

H	D	N
O	O	U
G	R	G

A	D	I
A	M	L
R	O	L

C	O	W
H	L	N
S	I	F

70

Starting with the gray 'P', create a connected path that visits every square and spells each of the animals listed under the puzzle. You can connect letters horizontally (↔) or vertically (↕).

P	A	N	N	K	A	N	G	A	N
E	C	L	O	R	T	S	A	M	A
L	I	A	I	I	R	O	R	S	T
B	Y	D	P	C	E	T	O	U	E
U	C	O	R	H	E	A	O	R	E
G	S	O	R	C	D	B	X	E	Q
D	O	C	G	U	R	L	I	A	U
I	K	S	I	A	E	V	A	Y	E
L	A	H	K	N	Y	N	E	B	K
E	Y	A	R	A	L	X	M	O	N

BEAVER

BAT

CROCODILE

DEER

IGUANA

KANGAROO

LADYBUG

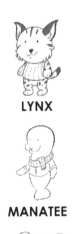

LYNX

MANATEE

MONKEY

OSTRICH

PELICAN

QUAIL

SCORPION

SHARK

XERUS

YAK

For both sets of three baskets, pick a letter from the first basket, then second, then third. Using those three letters in order, can you write down at least ten words for both sets of baskets?

The grid below contains only animals. Numbers correspond to a particular letter. A few number-letter combinations are provided. Can you complete the rest? All letters A to Z are used at least once.

Solve the clues to unlock the letters for the hidden phrase.
You can also use a partially completed phrase to help solve the clues.
Work the puzzle back and forth to find all the letters.

1	2	3	4	█	5	6	7	8	9	█	10	11	12	13	█
14	15	█	16	17	18	19	20	21	22	23	█	24	25	26	27
28	29	30	31	32	█	33	34	35	36	37	38	39	█	40	41
42	43	44	█	45	46	47	█	48	49	█					

---

27 16 12 42
molten rock

24 13 33 20
direction the sun sets

4 47 10
small floor covering

17 41 1
play with this

---

2 7 37 29
opposite of under

32 44 3 23
sticky crafting object

38 30 18
____ in a chair

19 35 6
frozen water

---

43 25 46 31
large cat with a mane

36 14 28 8
three-dimensional square

39 34 5
provides daylight

49 26 22
not young

---

21 15
opposite of down

48 11 9 40 45
needs to be cleaned

74

Can you figure out the phrase for each of these word puzzles?
Consider how the words are written, the number of times, their direction, and placement.

1 **SHOES** **SHOES**	2 LEAGUE	3 **RECORD**
4 GEGS GEGS / SGEG GGSE / SEGG ESGG / EGSG GESG	5 **BOOK** **DUE**	6 **COLOR**
7 RIGHT RIGHT / THE / CORNER / RIGHT RIGHT	8 **TIME**	9 PIGGY RIDE

1	2	3
Pair of shoes		
4	5	6
7	8	9

Drop letters in the appropriate square of each column (↕) to make words and reveal a quote.
Two words in each puzzle have been done to help get you started.

Puzzle 1 — letter tiles (top to bottom per column):

| I̶ O Y O | F N T̶ O | U S̶ | I T | M H F C | P A U A | N R N T | O | V T J̶ D | E O U̶ O | T O M | E F I R̶ | T N N̶ I | T N E̶ | D Y̶ |

Given entries: J O U R N E Y · I T S

Puzzle 2 — letter tiles (top to bottom per column):

| R̶ O T | S̶ W H | S̶ E N E | P̶ R | L L̶ O C | S N̶ O H | S S̶ O | E̶ I A O | N S | G I I L̶ | E̶ S | Y S̶ G | O Y S̶ | O O̶ R N̶ | U U | R | I N |

Given entries: L E S S O N · R E S P O N S E

76

Focus Activities

The greatest inventions that ever existed
are with us today because someone persisted.
Their inventors stayed focused and fully determined.
Their failures were setbacks but never were burdens.

Work through the small stuff — the tiniest things.
Seek the root of a problem to give your thoughts wings.
There's a challenge ahead. Wipe the sweat from your brow.
Pay close attention. Look carefully, now.

Use the picture below to answer the questions.

Circle the sheep which only appears one time.
Put squares around the sheep which appears most frequently.
Cross out the sheep which appear exactly five times.

How many unique kinds of sheep are there?

Follow the path of hamsters to the finish!
You may move horizontally (↔) or vertically (↕) but must follow this order:

1 2 3 4

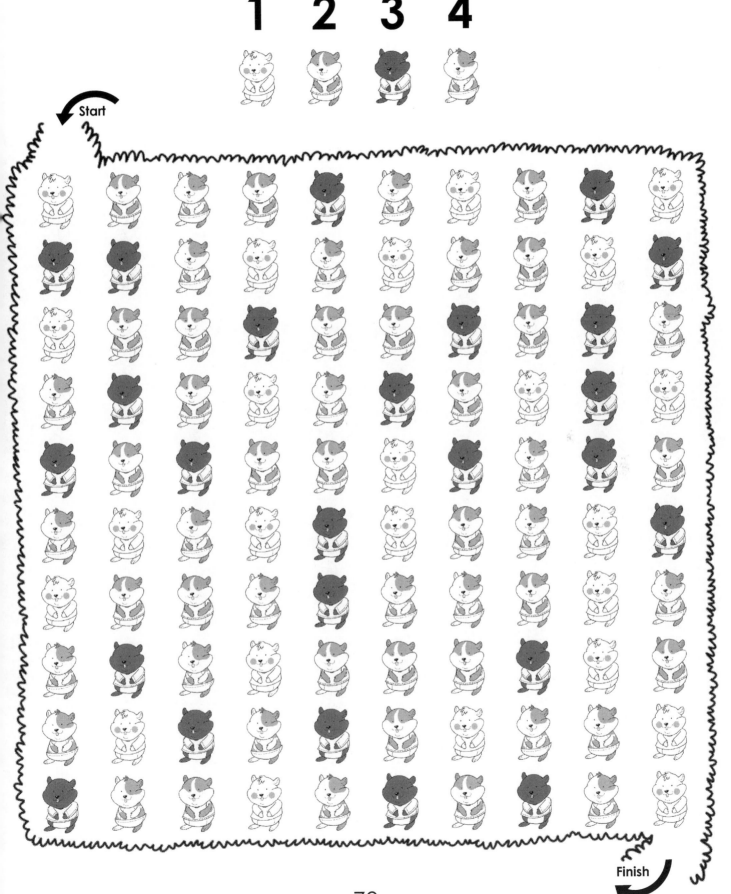

Start

Finish

Connect the dots!

Count the objects hidden in the drawing.

Circle the two identical drawings.

Find and circle the hidden four-leaf clover.
There is only one!

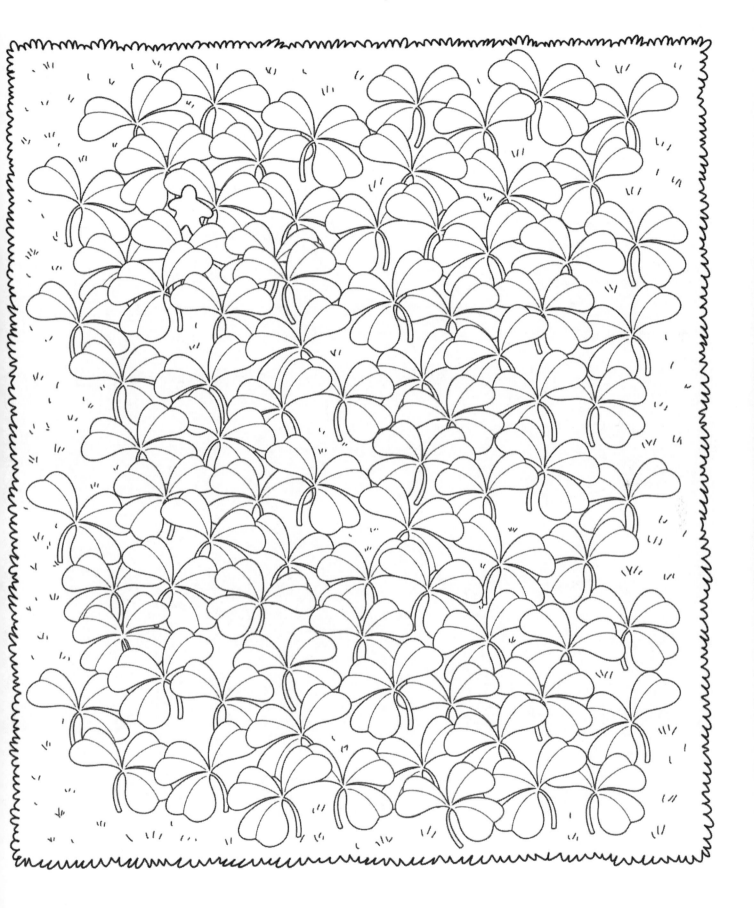

Fill in the triangles to reveal a picture!

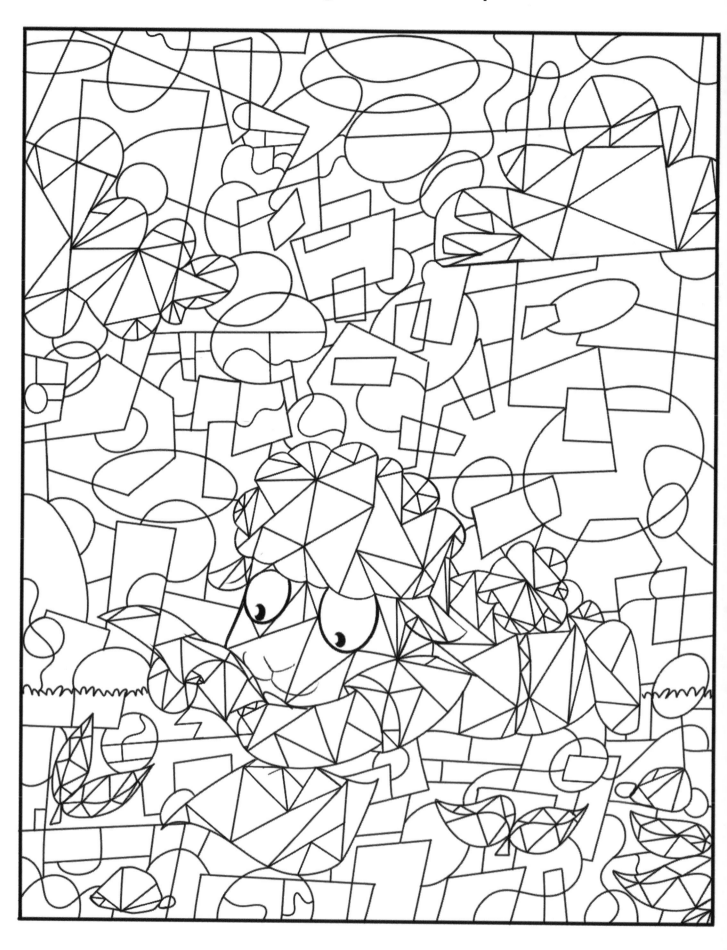

For the grids on the left, find and outline the clusters shown to the right.

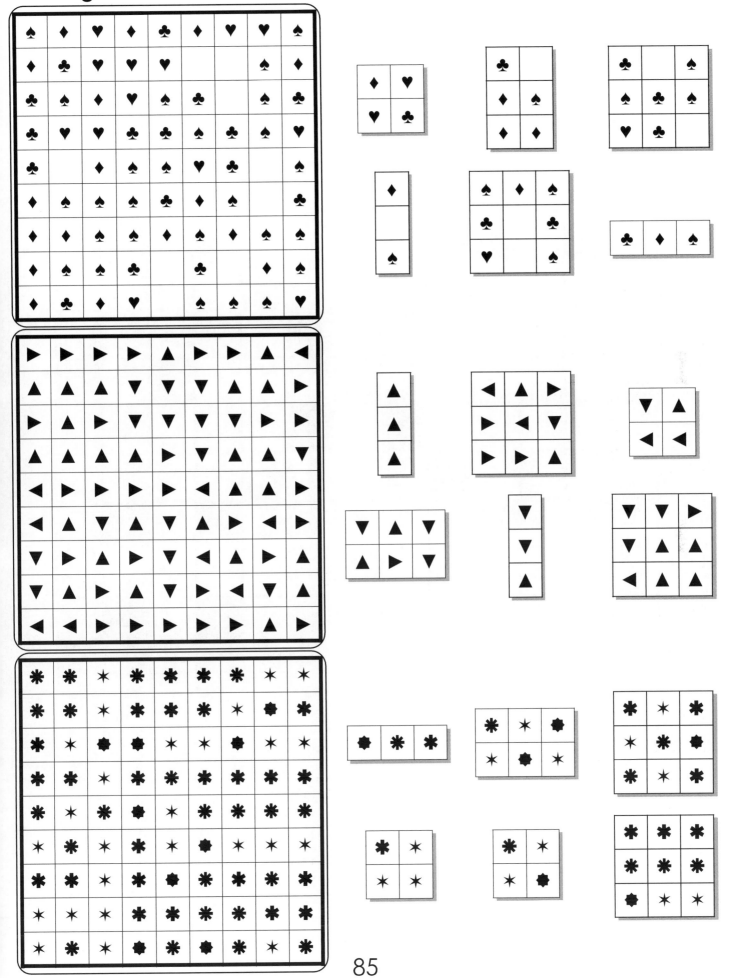

85

Fit the provided numbers into the grid.
A few answers have been filled in to help you get started.

3 digit	4 digit	5 digit		6 digit	
056	0717	07439	76285	037868	351563
057	0775	09462	76530	076062	357378
086	0909	10004	77530	082714	366905
088	5030	13981	85333	102143	502588
383	6010	18734	87666	~~170064~~	518464
437	6655	26474	93305	203983	700201
484	6691	33037	96635	328812	719602
534	8618	~~69656~~	98007	332889	992707

Can you navigate the maze?

Start

Finish

Reveal the hidden picture by coloring in squares in the correct location
The coordinates show where each
piece fits into the grid.

88

Hidden pictures!

Can you find?

Can you find and circle 16 differences between these pictures?

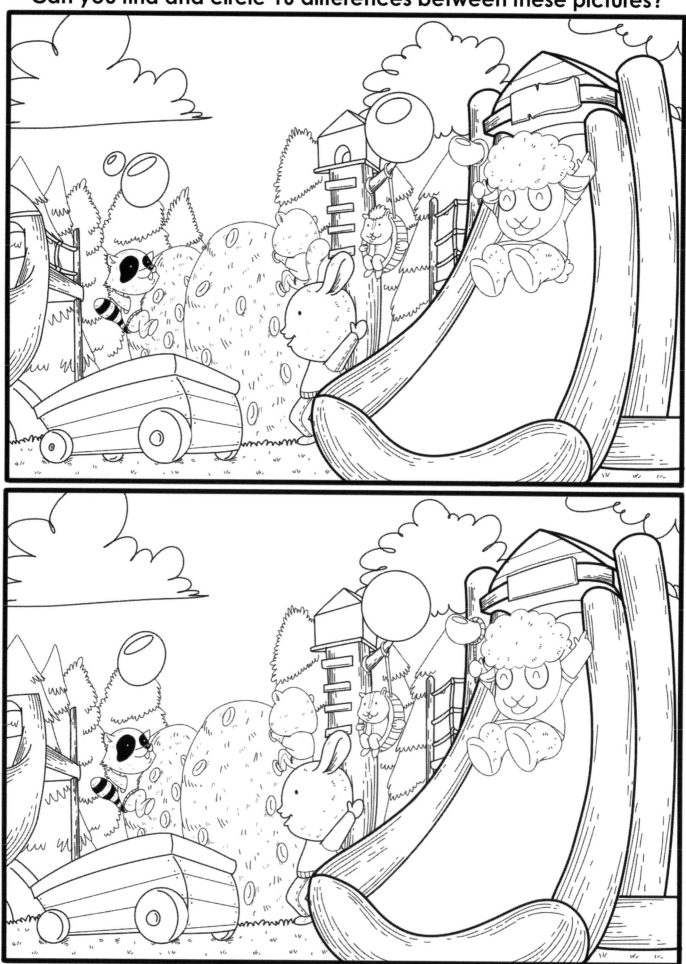

Two-Player Games

You can set your own limits. Go out and explore!
If you don't take a leap, then how else will you soar?
"I can" and "I can't" are both possibly true—
that outcome, however, is all up to you.

The games you play here seem simple enough,
though as you'll soon see, the decisions are tough.
But at the same time, they're tremendously fun.
You'll need an opponent—recruit someone!

91

Balloon Pop

GOAL

Pop the last balloon.

RULES

1. Taking turns, each player may pop one, two, or three balloons (mark an 'x' or color it in).
2. If you pop the last balloon, you win!

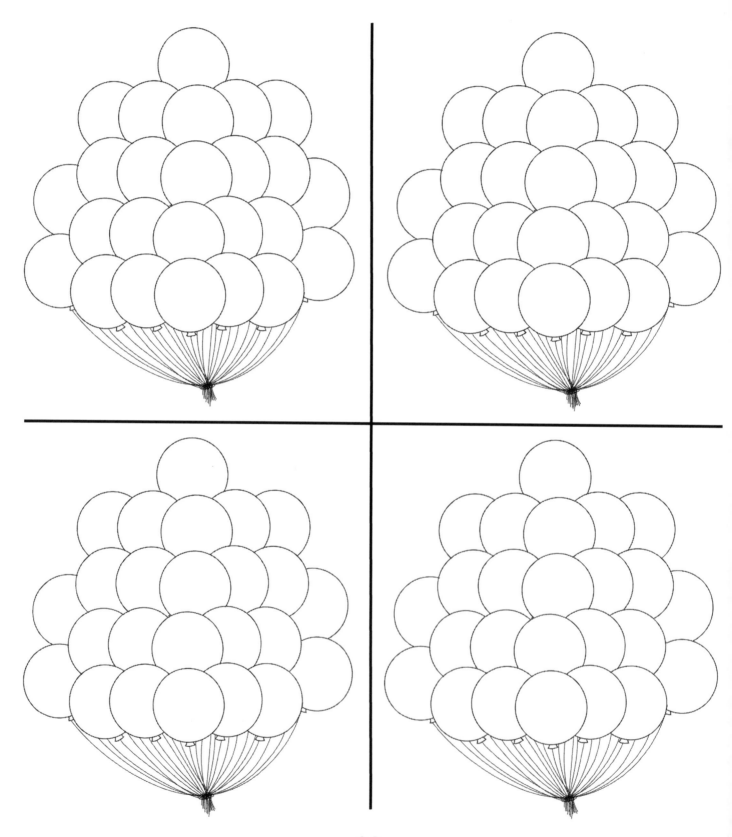

Hackenbush

Be the last player to take a turn.

RULES

1. Taking turns, eliminate any line segment by crossing it out. After that, any line that can no longer be traced back to the ground is also crossed out.
2. The last player able to make a move wins.

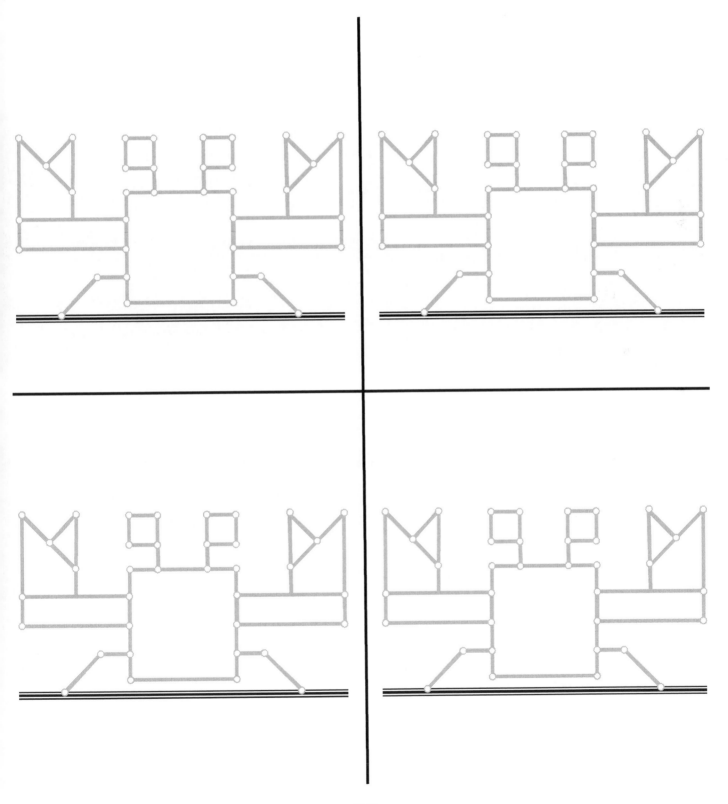

Honeycomb

GOAL

Trap your opponent.

RULES

1. One player draws solid dots while the other player draws open dots.
2. Each player chooses one hexagon as a starting location and draws their dot.
3. Taking turns, each player moves their dot as far as they want in a straight line in any one of the six directions. During movement you cannot change directions. You are also not allowed to move through your opponent's dot or a filled-in hexagon (both block any further movement in that direction).
4. Place your dot in only the hexagon where you ended your movement, then completely fill in the hexagon you just left.
5. Play continues until one player is unable to make a legal move. The other player wins.

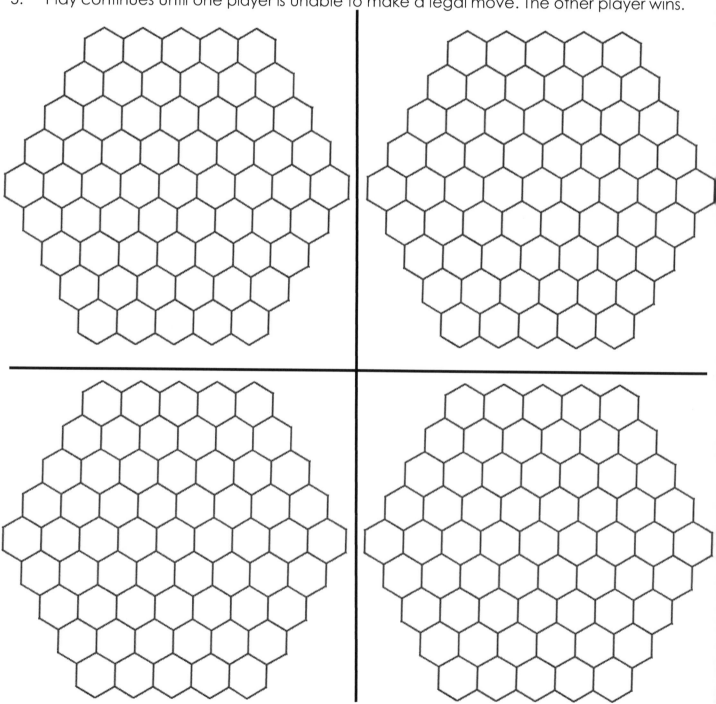

94

Getaway

GOAL
Have the most dots in the gray border spaces.

RULES
1. One player draws solid dots while the other player draws open dots.
2. Taking turns, move into one open box in any direction, including diagonally, then place your dot.
3. You are allowed to jump over dots, but only if they are your color.
4. You may jump over multiple dots of your color by continuing the jump in the same direction until an open box is reached.
5. You can only reach the gray border spaces by jumping over your own color.
6. If you cannot make a legal play you must pass.
7. Play continues until there are no more legal moves. The winner is the person with the most dots in the gray area.

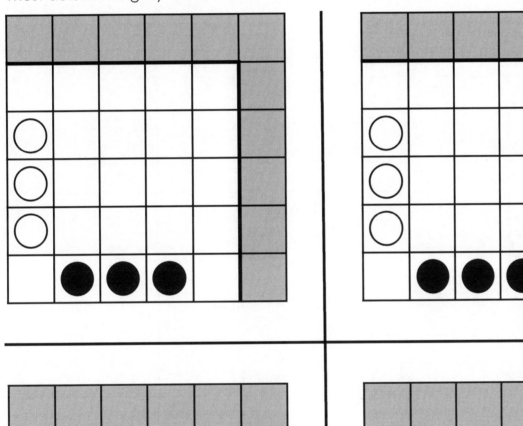

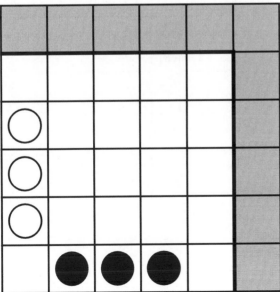

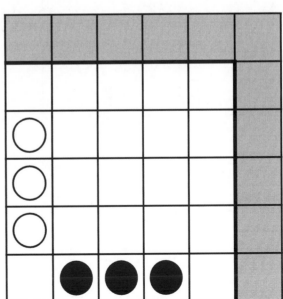

Leapfrog

GOAL

Have the most dots at game end.

RULES

1. One player draws solid dots while the other player draws open dots.
2. Taking turns, jump over the other player into an empty box in any direction, including diagonally. You are allowed to make a chain of jumps on a single turn, if possible.
3. Each time you land a jump, draw your dot.
4. If you cannot make a legal move, the other player fills in the remaining boxes.
5. The winner is the person with the most dots belonging to them once the grid is filled.

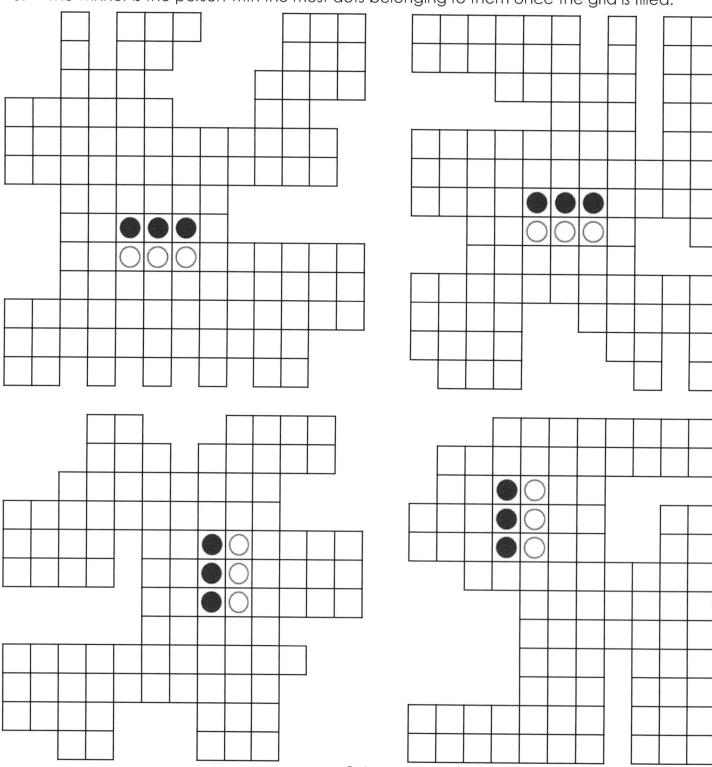

Trio

GOAL
Have the highest sum after some numbers are crossed out.

RULES
The game is played in two phases. Seed and cross out.

SEED PHASE
1. Using different colors, take turns placing a 1, 2, or 3 in your own color in any open box.
2. You must use all values 1, 2, and 3 before you can repeat the sequence.
3. Continue until the board is full (players should both have six of each value 1, 2, and 3).

CROSS OUT PHASE
1. Taking turns, cross out a chain containing values 1, 2, and 3 from boxes touching vertically ($\updownarrow$) or horizontally ($\leftrightarrow$).
2. The cross-out marking is allowed to turn and number order does not matter (for example, you could cross out 3-1-2).
3. Play continues until no more cross-out markings can legally be made. The winner is the player with the highest sum of remaining numbers in their color.

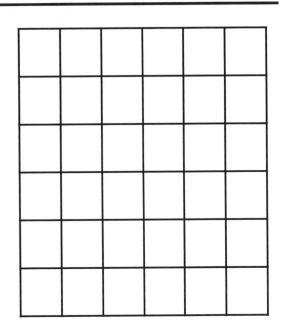

Example of end game. White wins 10 to 2.

97

Network

GOAL

Have the largest network of connected lines.

RULES

1. One player owns the solid dots (●) while the other player owns the open dots (○).
2. Taking turns, connect two of your dots with a horizontal (↔) or vertical (↕) line segment.
3. Lines may not cross each other.
4. If you cannot play you must skip your turn.
5. Play until no more moves are possible.
6. The winner is the player with the most line segments within their largest network of connected lines.

98

Intersection

GOAL

Have the most groups of three dots in a row.

RULES

1. One player draws solid dots while the other player draws open dots.
2. Taking turns, draw your dot at any location where lines intersect; however, the first move by the first player may not be to the middle point.
3. If you after placing your dot, you have three in a row in your color in any direction, including diagonally, place one extra dot at any other intersection. You may only place an extra dot at most once per turn.
4. For any group of three, only one dot may be shared with another group of three (two groups of three may share a single dot).
5. The winner is the player with the most groups of three.

Scoring tip: first score horizontally (↔), then vertically (↕), then diagonally to help avoid errors.

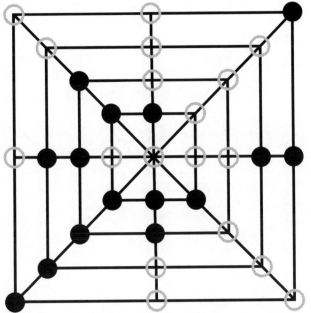

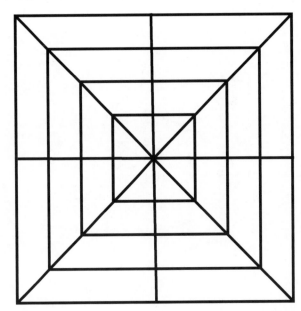

Example of end game. White wins 7 to 4.

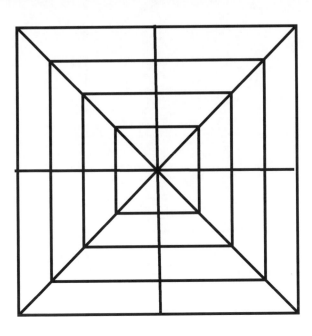

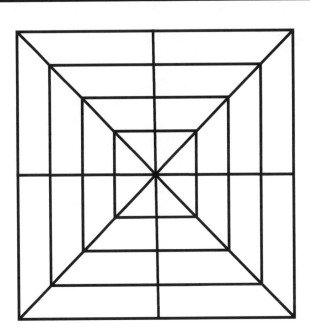

Line Runner

GOAL
Force your opponent to be unable to make a legal move.

RULES

1. One player draws solid dots while the other player draws open dots.
2. As their starting position, each player chooses one location where lines intersect and draws their dot.
3. On your turn, place your writing utensil on the dot you drew most recently. Trace the line going as far and turning as much as you would like.
4. During tracing you cannot move through occupied intersections.
5. End tracing at any unoccupied intersection and draw your dot.
6. The first player who cannot complete their turn loses.

Boxed In

Close in the most board squares with your own color lines.

RULES

1. Play in two different colors.
2. Taking turns, place any of the following six figures completely inside the board boundary without any part overlapping an already placed figure. You are allowed to rotate these figures or use their mirror images (more simply, draw a square with two protruding lines).

3. Play until it is not possible to place any more figures.
4. The player with more board squares completely enclosed by only their color wins.

101

Point to Point

GOAL

Make the most connections.

RULES

1. One player owns solid triangles while the other owns open triangles.
2. Taking turns, draw a line from one open corner of one of your triangles to an open tip of any asterisk (✳). Lines may be long or curvy but may never cross other lines or objects.
3. If you cannot make a legal play you must pass.
4. Play continues until there are no more legal moves. The winner is the person with the most connections.

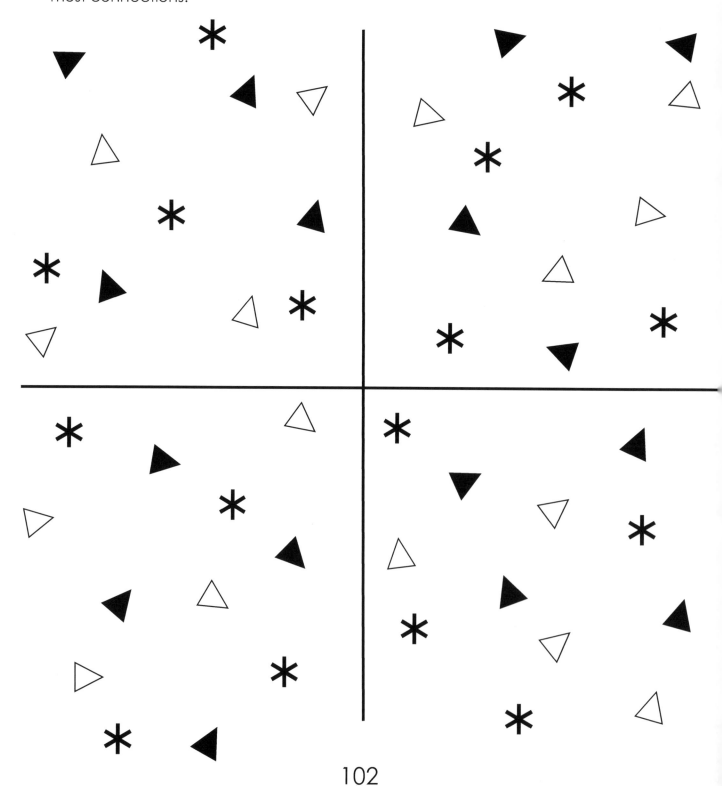

102

End of the Line

GOAL

Block in your opponent.

RULES

1. One player starts at the 'A' dot while the other player starts at 'B'.
2. Taking turns, draw a line which connects four dots (thus drawing three line segments).
3. Each line segment may connect to dots horizontally (↔), vertically (↕), or diagonally.
4. Lines may cross, but no dot can be connected more than once.
5. Play continues until one player is blocked in.

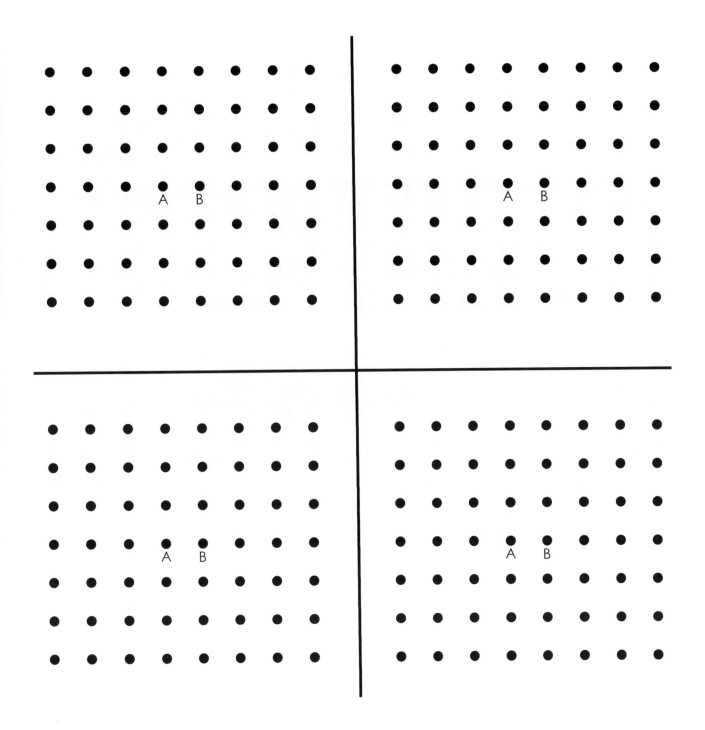

Eclipse

GOAL

Control three spaces in a row.

RULES

1.   Play in two different colors.
2.   Taking turns, fill in an empty circle of your choice. If you fill in a larger circle, color over any smaller circles, even if they already contain the opponent color (you eclipse them).
3.   The player with the largest colored circle controls the space.
4.   Each player may only color in at most two circles of each size (coloring a larger circle does not consume your smaller circles pieces as you fill those in). The player supply below the board can help keep track of circles used. Color in supply circles as you use them in the play area.
5.   You win if you are the first player to control three spaces in a row in any direction.

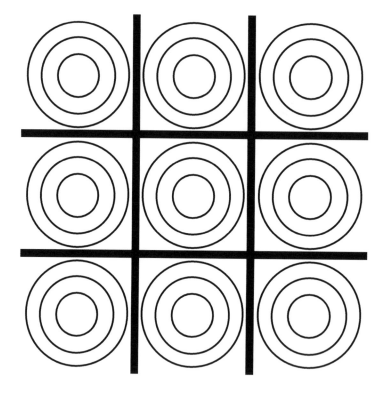

Player A supply   Player B supply

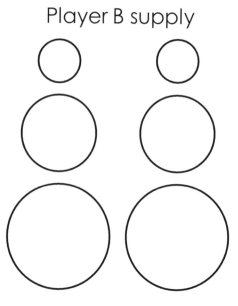

Answers

Did other kids find this book easy or hard?
That's not your concern. You can let down your guard.

Did you improve and get better today?
Carefully listen. Here's what I say:
"No matter my growth, whether massive or small,
I'm proud of myself since I gave it my all!"

Because, let me tell you a plain, simple truth:
you may try and fail, but you can't till you do.
Progress is powerful. Never forget
that you really can do it, just maybe not yet .

Match the folded and cut paper with the unfolded paper shapes. Write your answers in the gray boxes.

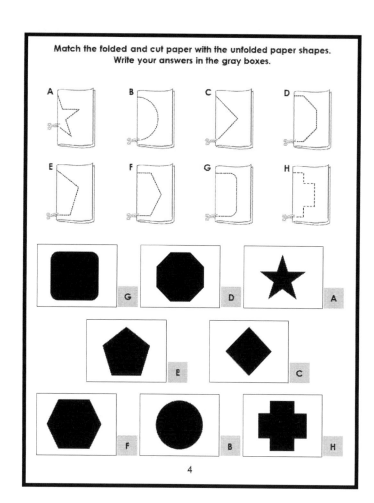

For each of the puzzles below, circle the piece which would best complete the missing square.

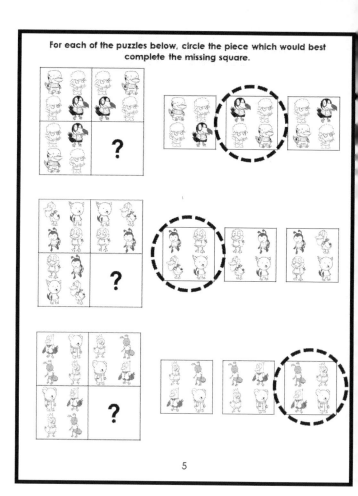

Bison got separated from her herd. Can you help her get back?

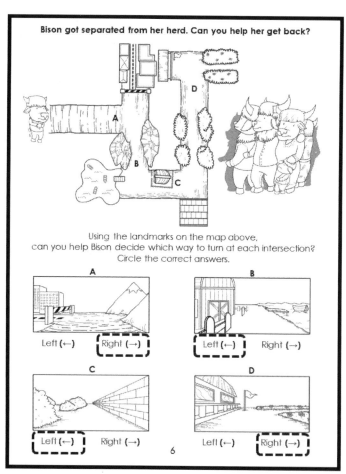

Using the landmarks on the map above, can you help Bison decide which way to turn at each intersection? Circle the correct answers.

For each puzzle, connect the two black dots while drawing a continuous line that passes through every gray dot. The line can only go horizontally (↔) or vertically (↕).

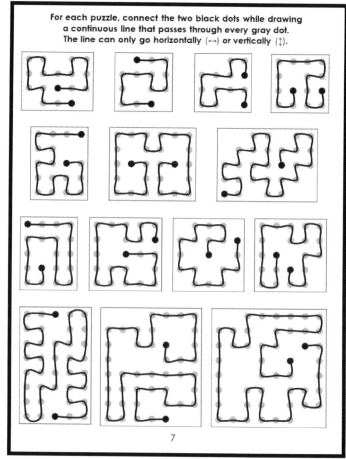

Alternative solutions for some of these puzzles are possible.

106

Draw a horizontal (↔) or vertical (↕) line to match one bird to one feather.
Lines cannot cross over birds, feathers, or each other.
Connect all birds and feathers.

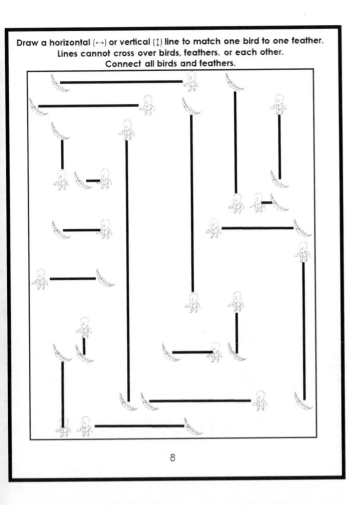

8

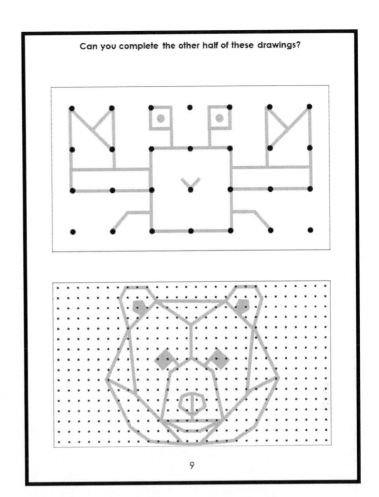

9

For each shape, make a continuous line that stays on the gray path
and passes through all the dots. Begin on any dot you choose.
No retracing over lines, but you may pass through dots more than once.

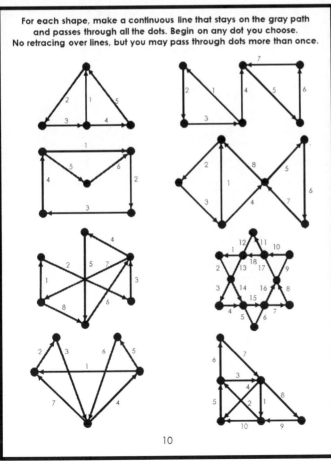

10

Each of these knots is different.
Count the number of ropes in each knot.

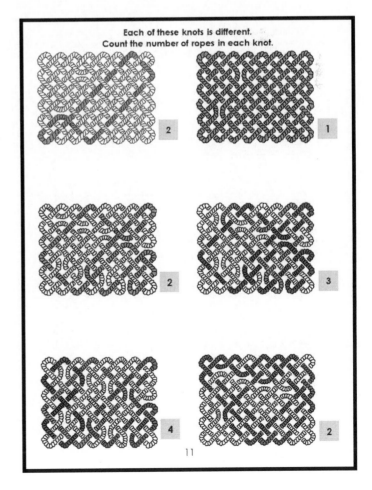

11

Alternative solutions for these puzzles are possible.

107

How many eggs are there?

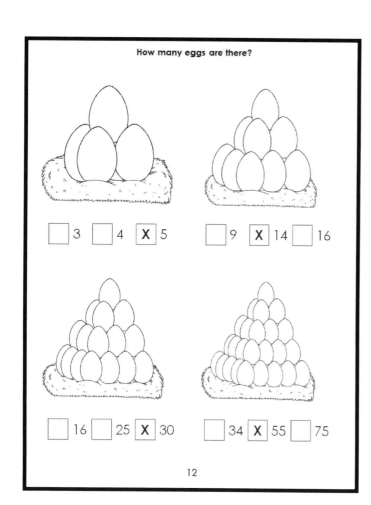

☐ 3 ☐ 4 ☒ 5   ☐ 9 ☒ 14 ☐ 16

☐ 16 ☐ 25 ☒ 30   ☐ 34 ☒ 55 ☐ 75

12

Which way will the gray gear spin? Circle the correct answer.

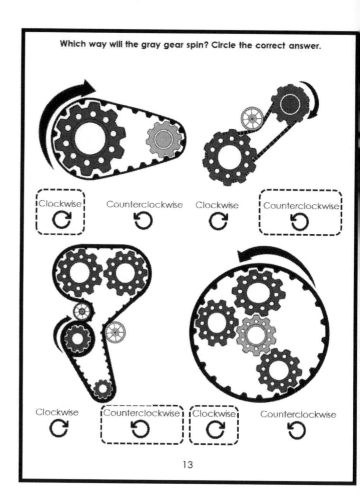

Clockwise   Counterclockwise   Clockwise   Counterclockwise

Clockwise   Counterclockwise   Clockwise   Counterclockwise

13

For each puzzle, connect the two black dots while drawing a continuous line that passes through every gray dot. The line can only go horizontally (↔) or vertically (↕).

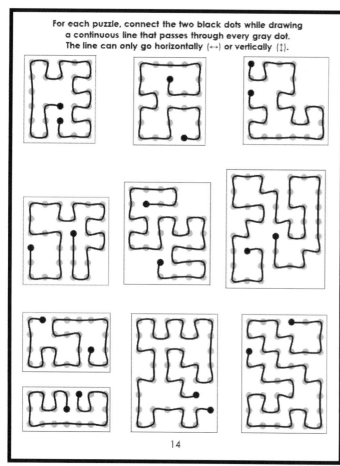

14

For each puzzle below, make three straight lines which create four animal groupings.

Each group should contain one of each of these animals:

Each group should contain one of each of these animals:

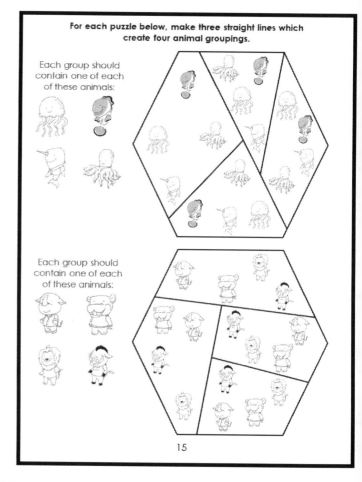

15

Alternative solutions for some of these puzzles are possible.

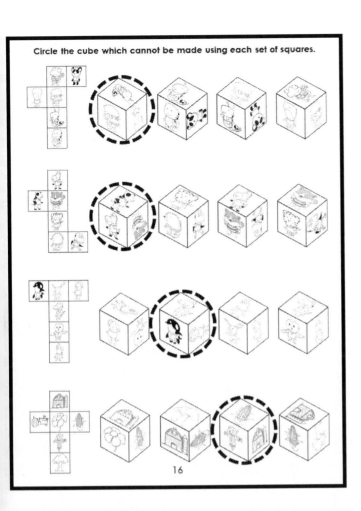

Circle the cube which cannot be made using each set of squares.

16

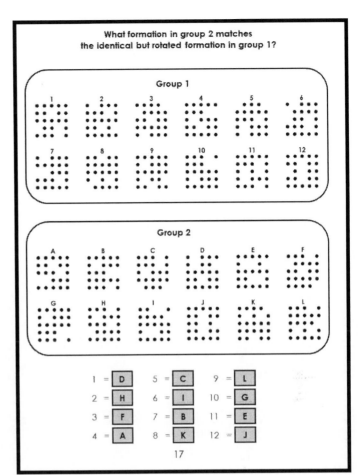

What formation in group 2 matches
the identical but rotated formation in group 1?

Group 1

Group 2

1 = D	5 = C	9 = L
2 = H	6 = I	10 = G
3 = F	7 = B	11 = E
4 = A	8 = K	12 = J

17

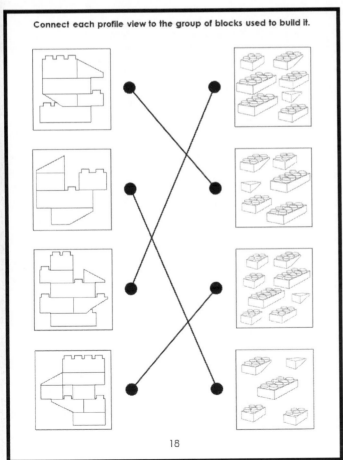

Connect each profile view to the group of blocks used to build it.

18

Use the following set of blocks to solve each puzzle.

The first one has been completed as an example.

19

Fun with lines!
One of these is not possible. Can you figure out which one?

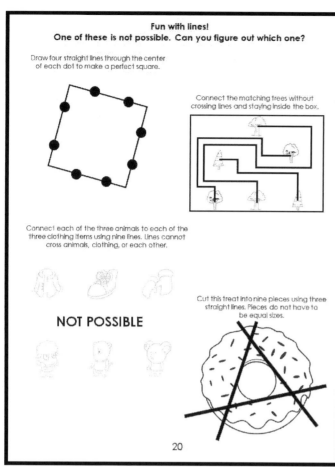

Draw four straight lines through the center of each dot to make a perfect square.

Connect the matching trees without crossing lines and staying inside the box.

Connect each of the three animals to each of the three clothing items using nine lines. Lines cannot cross animals, clothing, or each other.

NOT POSSIBLE

Cut this treat into nine pieces using three straight lines. Pieces do not have to be equal sizes.

20

Alternative solutions for the treat problem are possible.

Can you find the bush where Squirrel hid her acorns?
Begin at the star. Move around the map using the clues in order.

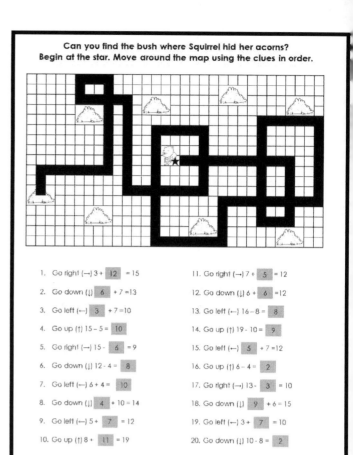

1. Go right (→) 3 + 12 = 15
2. Go down (↓) 6 + 7 = 13
3. Go left (←) 3 + 7 = 10
4. Go up (↑) 15 − 5 = 10
5. Go right (→) 15 − 6 = 9
6. Go down (↓) 12 − 4 = 8
7. Go left (←) 6 + 4 = 10
8. Go down (↓) 4 + 10 = 14
9. Go left (←) 5 + 7 = 12
10. Go up (↑) 8 + 11 = 19

11. Go right (→) 7 + 5 = 12
12. Go down (↓) 6 + 6 = 12
13. Go left (←) 16 − 8 = 8
14. Go up (↑) 19 − 10 = 9
15. Go left (←) 5 + 7 = 12
16. Go up (↑) 6 − 4 = 2
17. Go right (→) 13 − 3 = 10
18. Go down (↓) 9 + 6 = 15
19. Go left (←) 3 + 7 = 10
20. Go down (↓) 10 − 8 = 2

22

Spider caught lots of flies but can only eat three!
For each spiderweb, find the highest possible total value of flies. Start anywhere and collect three flies by following the webbed path. No jumping or going back over a path twice.

23

Lambie is looking for 24, his favorite number!
In each of the grids below there is only one time four numbers in a two-by-two square add up to 24. Can you find each of them?

4	1	6	8	4	4	6	1
1	1	2	6	2	1	4	6
5	4	1	7	1	4	3	6
2	6	7	**6**	**6**	8	6	7
4	1	1	**8**	**4**	7	6	3
5	5	2	4	2	5	6	4
1	8	9	3	8	5	9	7
2	6	5	1	7	8	9	7

5	8	4	6	6	1	1	1
7	9	2	8	3	8	4	3
1	4	1	6	5	2	6	9
8	**9**	7	1	4	8	9	1
5	**2**	7	4	8	8	1	4
5	5	3	2	7	2	2	9
4	2	1	2	8	9	4	2
4	7	1	9	2	2	5	4

2	8	**9**	**4**	3	8	6	7
1	1	**5**	**6**	5	6	3	9
6	6	6	6	9	7	3	4
5	9	9	9	5	8	2	5
7	8	2	3	3	6	3	5
1	9	6	1	9	9	8	2
7	4	3	1	5	6	7	9
7	3	1	9	1	1	8	1

4	5	2	1	4	1	6	1
5	4	9	4	4	5	7	1
6	6	1	9	2	8	1	3
9	1	4	1	5	9	1	2
6	2	5	1	5	9	1	2
3	2	2	5	7	1	**6**	**8**
2	2	2	2	9	8	**5**	**5**
5	5	5	8	2	1	9	7

24

110

Each block in a pyramid is the sum of the two numbers below it.
Can you complete each pyramid?

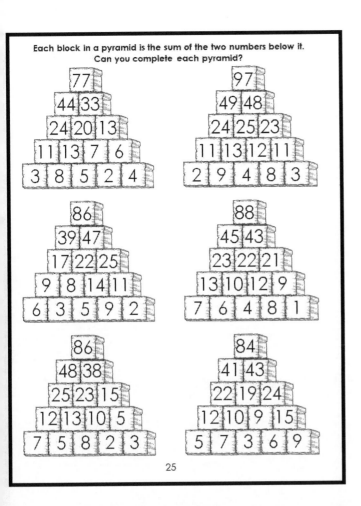

25

Within every large square, each row (↔), column (↕), and mini-grid must contain the numbers 1, 2, 3, and 4.

26

Which animal is the heaviest? Which is the lightest?

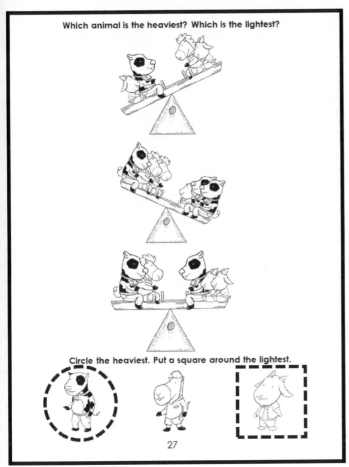

Circle the heaviest. Put a square around the lightest.

27

Fill in the gray squares with the correct number to make each equation true.

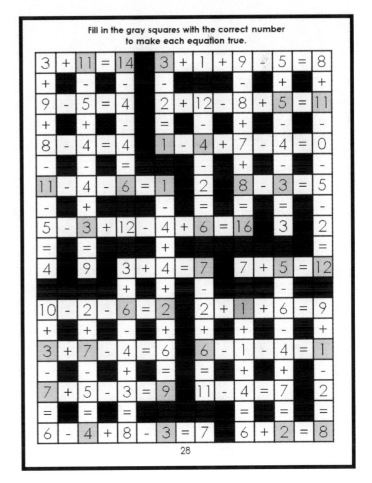

28

Orangutan is looking for a specific number of bananas.
Find the path of numbers that add up to the sum at the exit arrow.
For each puzzle, start at the top left banana,
then step down (↓) or right (→) with each move.

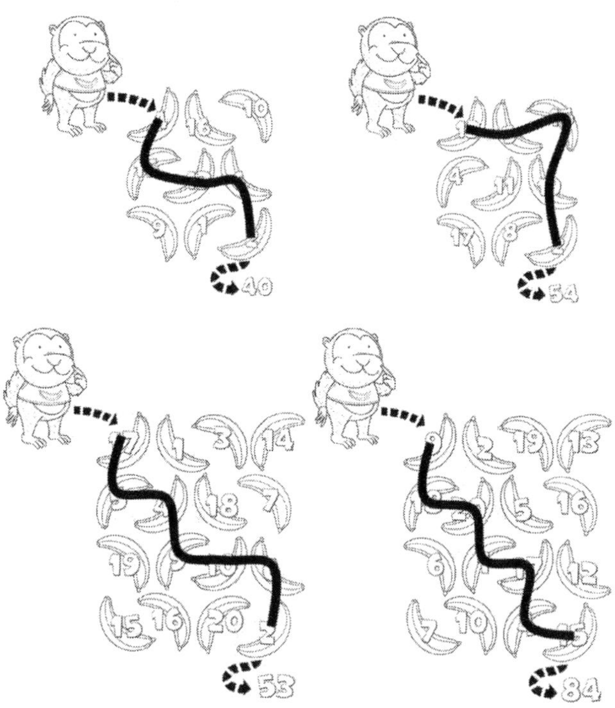

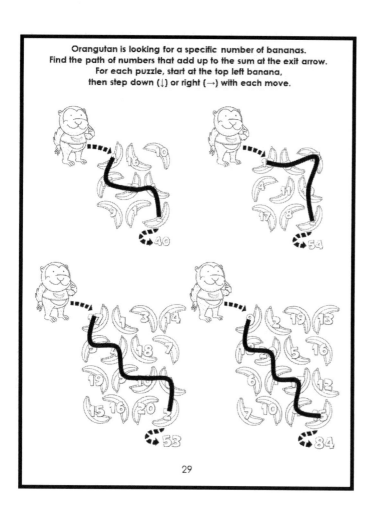

40
54
53
84

29

Within every large square, each row (↔), column (↕), and mini-grid must contain the numbers 1, 2, 3, 4, 5, and 6.

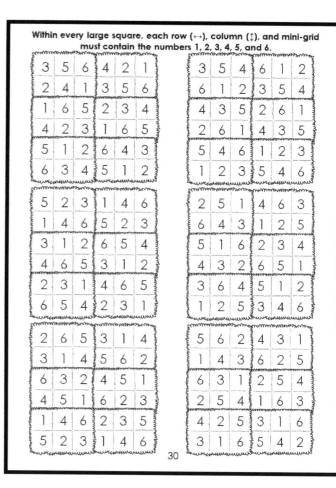

3	5	6	4	2	1
2	4	1	3	5	6
1	6	5	2	3	4
4	2	3	1	6	5
5	1	2	6	4	3
6	3	4	5	1	2

3	5	4	6	1	2
6	1	2	3	5	4
4	3	5	2	6	1
2	6	1	4	3	5
5	4	6	1	2	3
1	2	3	5	4	6

5	2	3	1	4	6
1	4	6	5	2	3
3	1	2	6	5	4
4	6	5	3	1	2
2	3	1	4	6	5
6	5	4	2	3	1

2	5	1	4	6	3
6	4	3	1	2	5
5	1	6	2	3	4
4	3	2	6	5	1
3	6	4	5	1	2
1	2	5	3	4	6

2	6	5	3	1	4
3	1	4	5	6	2
6	3	2	4	5	1
4	5	1	6	2	3
1	4	6	2	3	5
5	2	3	1	4	6

5	6	2	4	3	1
1	4	3	6	2	5
6	3	1	2	5	4
2	5	4	1	6	3
4	2	5	3	1	6
3	1	6	5	4	2

30

Each puzzle must contain all numbers 1 to 9.
Some numbers have been provided.
Fill in the gray boxes to make the equations true.

9	+	6	+	3	18
-	■	+	■	+	
8	-	5	+	2	5
+	■	-	■	+	
7	+	4	-	1	10
8		7		6	

2	+	8	-	4	6
+	■	+	■	+	
7	-	1	-	5	1
-	■	-	■	-	
3	+	6	-	9	0
6		3		0	

7	-	4	-	1	2
+	■	+	■	+	
2	+	9	-	5	6
-	■	-	■	-	
8	-	3	+	6	11
1		10		0	

9	+	8	+	7	24
+	■	+	■	+	
6	+	4	+	2	12
+	■	+	■	+	
5	+	3	+	1	9
20		15		10	

9	-	8	-	1	0
-	■	+	■	+	
7	-	3	-	4	0
-	■	-	■	-	
2	+	6	-	5	3
0		5		0	

6	+	1	+	8	15
+	■	+	■	+	
7	+	5	+	3	15
+	■	+	■	+	
2	+	9	+	4	15
15		15		15	

31

Alternative solutions for the bottom right puzzle are possible.

In this grid are hidden 63 addition and subtraction problems.
The equations may be positioned: ➡ ⬇ ⬊ ⬈
Can you find them all and complete the equation?
One is marked to help get you started. Not all numbers will be used.

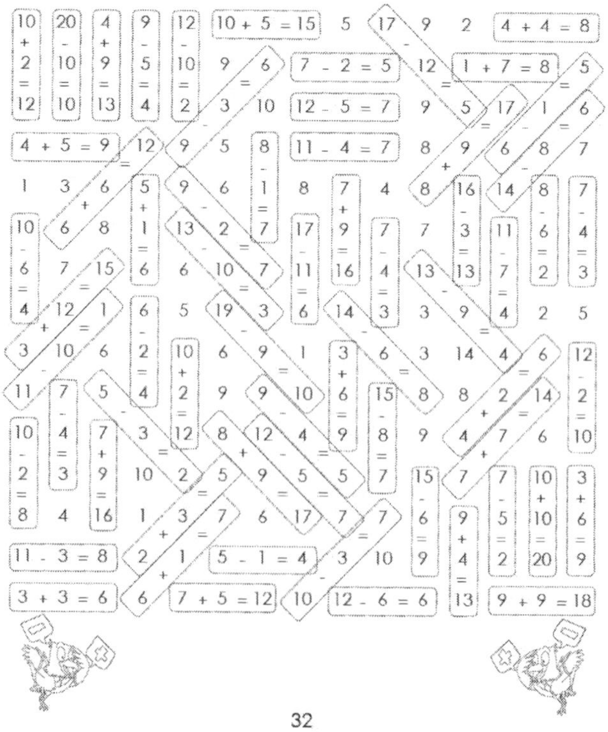

10 + 5 = 15
4 + 4 = 8
7 - 2 = 5
1 + 7 = 8
12 - 5 = 7
4 + 5 = 9
11 - 4 = 7
11 - 3 = 8
5 - 1 = 4
3 + 3 = 6
7 + 5 = 12
12 - 6 = 6
9 + 9 = 18

32

Fill in each grid with numbers to make a connected path.
Count by a different number as shown above each grid.
You can connect numbers horizontally (↔) and vertically (↕).

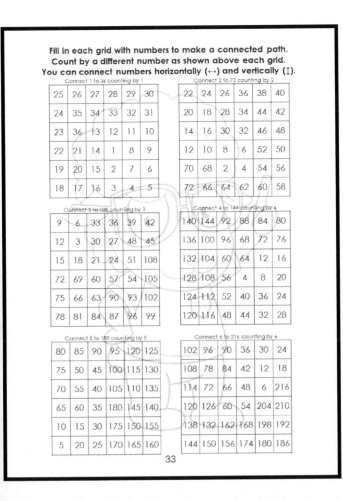

Connect 1 to 36 counting by 1

25	26	27	28	29	30
24	35	34	33	32	31
23	36	13	12	11	10
22	21	14	1	8	9
19	20	15	2	7	6
18	17	16	3	4	5

Connect 2 to 72 counting by 2

22	24	26	36	38	40
20	18	28	34	44	42
14	16	30	32	46	48
12	10	8	6	52	50
70	68	2	4	54	56
72	66	64	62	60	58

Connect 3 to 108 counting by 3

9	6	33	36	39	42
12	3	30	27	48	45
15	18	21	24	51	108
72	69	60	57	54	105
75	66	63	90	93	102
78	81	84	87	96	99

Connect 4 to 144 counting by 4

140	144	92	88	84	80
136	100	96	68	72	76
132	104	60	64	12	16
128	108	56	4	8	20
124	112	52	40	36	24
120	116	48	44	32	28

Connect 5 to 180 counting by 5

80	85	90	95	120	125
75	50	45	100	115	130
70	55	40	105	110	135
65	60	35	180	145	140
10	15	30	175	150	155
5	20	25	170	165	160

Connect 6 to 216 counting by 6

102	96	90	36	30	24
108	78	84	42	12	18
114	72	66	48	6	216
120	126	60	54	204	210
138	132	162	168	198	192
144	150	156	174	180	186

33

Find your way down through this math maze.
You can only exit a cell if a number in the tunnel matches the answer.
Beware of dead ends!

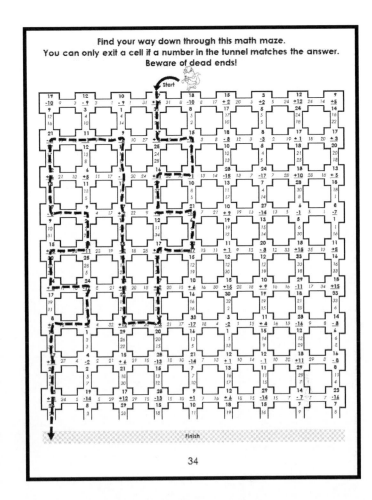

Start

Finish

34

Each animal represents a number from 1 to 10. Use the equations to figure out each animal's number. Write your answers in the gray boxes.

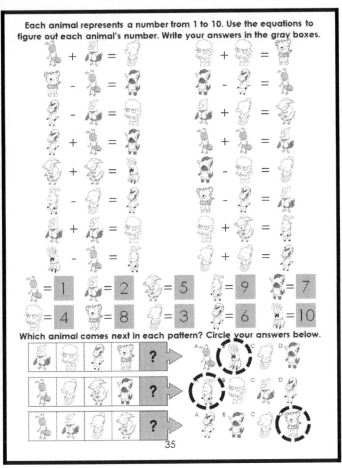

Which animal comes next in each pattern? Circle your answers below.

35

For each puzzle use all the available numbers one time. Your goal is to have the difference between connected circles all be unique numbers. The first one is completed as an example.

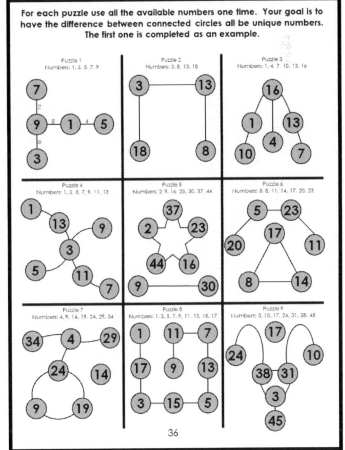

36

Alternative solutions for these puzzles are possible.

113

In each section, circle the animals that meet the conditions indicated.

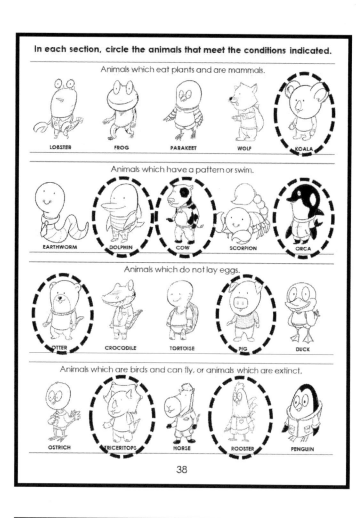

Animals which eat plants and are mammals.

LOBSTER FROG PARAKEET WOLF KOALA

Animals which have a pattern or swim.

EARTHWORM DOLPHIN COW SCORPION ORCA

Animals which do not lay eggs.

OTTER CROCODILE TORTOISE PIG DUCK

Animals which are birds and can fly, or animals which are extinct.

OSTRICH TRICERITOPS HORSE ROOSTER PENGUIN

38

Every day one animal is the leader and chooses the group play activity. Which animal is the group leader each day?

- Tortoise leads on a weekend day.
- Orangutan leads four days before Tiger.
- Camel leads between Lambie and Sloth.
- Tiger gets to lead on Fridays.
- Sloth and Lambie are leaders two days apart.
- Warthog is the leader three days after Camel.
- Lambie is the leader the day after Orangutan.

Can you draw lines to connect each animal to the day they are the leader?

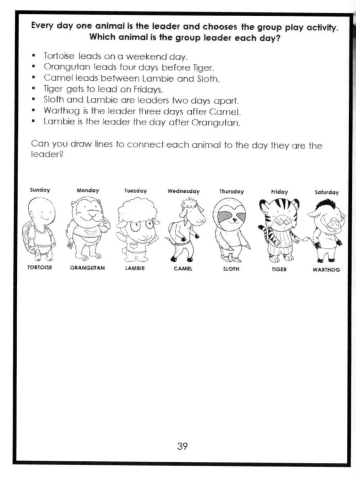

Sunday Monday Tuesday Wednesday Thursday Friday Saturday

TORTOISE ORANGUTAN LAMBIE CAMEL SLOTH TIGER WARTHOG

39

Where is Tiger hiding?

Using the map and clues provided below, circle the only spot on the map where Tiger could be hiding.

Clues:
- Tiger is hiding within one space of water.
- Tiger is not hiding within one space of a desert.
- Tiger is hiding within one space of a mountain.
- Tiger is not hiding within one space of a forest.
- Tiger is hiding in the grasslands.

water desert mountain forest grasslands

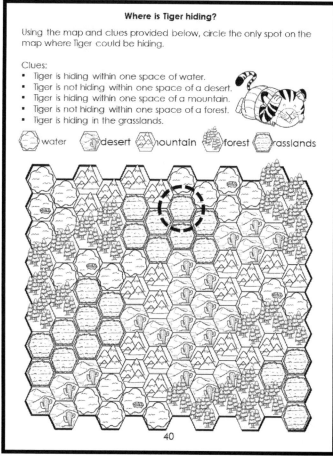

40

Can you connect each animal to their location?

- Peacock isn't in a corner, but Spider is.
- Leopard is the farthest distance from Giraffe, who is next to Turkey.
- Seal is in the same column (↕) as Mouse, who is in the same row (↔) as Fox.

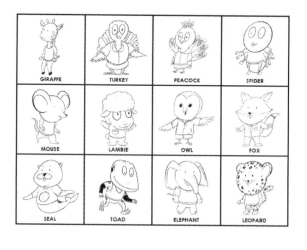

GIRAFFE TURKEY PEACOCK SPIDER

MOUSE LAMBIE OWL FOX

SEAL TOAD ELEPHANT LEOPARD

41

114

Fill in each grid so that each column (↕) and row (↔)
contains the numbers 1, 2, 3, and 4.
Boxes connected by a line mean the numbers are consecutive.
The absence of a line means numbers are not consecutive.

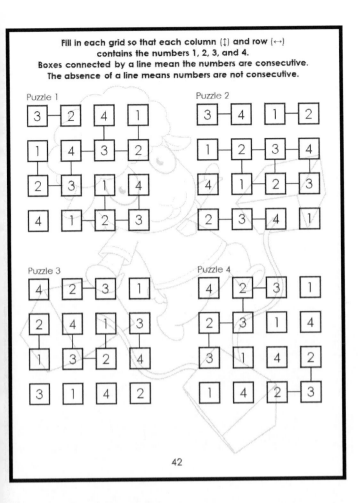

Fill in each grid so that each column (↕) and row (↔)
contains the numbers 1, 2, 3, and 4.
Pairs of numbers must satisfy the inequality signs of
greater than (>) and less than (<).

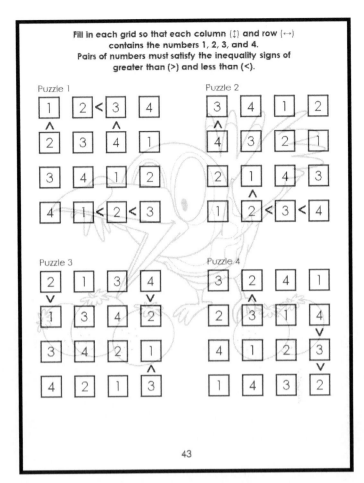

What day is it today?

- Piano lessons start in the prior week before the tennis tournament.
- There is no chess club today.
- Today is not an even day.
- Alpaca's tennis tournament is the last Saturday of the month.
- Today is a school day.
- Alpaca starts taking piano lessons in two weeks.
- Alpaca has chess club on Thursdays.

Can you use this calendar to figure out today's date?

Can you connect each animal to their location?

- Giraffe, Turkey, and Mouse are in the same row (↔).
- Lambie and Peacock are in opposite corners.
- Turkey, Giraffe, and Owl are next to Elephant.
- Peacock is next to Mouse.
- Fox and Seal are in the same row (↔).
- Lambie, Giraffe, and Spider are in the same column (↕).

115

Where does each animal live?

- Squirrel lives West of Lambie.
- Goat is neighbors with Skunk and Lambie.
- Raccoon lives in the Southeast.
- Horse lives in the Southern row.
- Cow lives directly East of Goat.
- Cat lives North of Raccoon and East of Lambie.
- Skunk lives East of Horse.
- Lambie lives in the Northern row.
- Pig lives South of Squirrel and West of Goat.

Can you draw a line from each animal to their house?

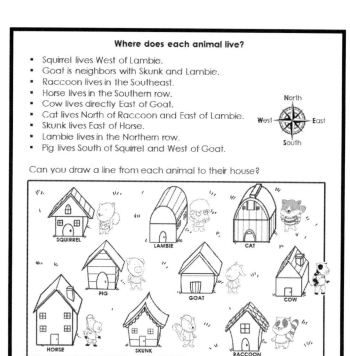

46

Where did Dog bury the bone?

Dog buried a bone somewhere on the island.
He gives you the following clues:

- It is not within two spaces of a hut.
- It is not in or next to a beach.
- It is within two spaces of a palm tree.
- It is next to, but not in a lake.
- It is next to a mountain.
- It is not next to the ocean.

jungle   scrubland   palm tree
mountain   beach   hut
lake   river   ocean

Can you use those clues to figure out where the bone is buried?
Circle the correct hexagon below.

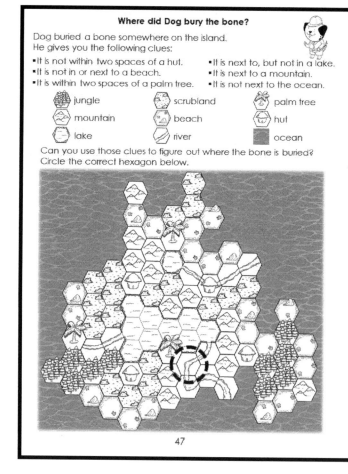

47

Connect the dots. Numbers show how many lines touch that dot. Draw lines horizontally (↔) or vertically (↕) only. There are two lines at most per dot. The first one is completed as an example.

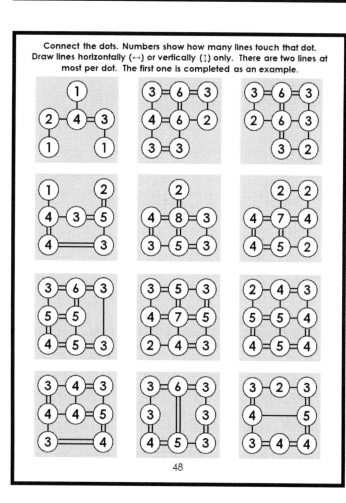

48

Can you connect each animal to their location?

- Toad and Leopard are in the same column (↕).
- Mouse is between Seal and Giraffe.
- Lambie and Leopard are as far apart as they can be.
- Turkey is in the same column (↕) as Peacock, who is in the same row (↔) as Elephant, who is in the same column (↕) as Spider, who is in the same row (↔) as Leopard.
- Fox is next to Giraffe.
- Mouse and Spider are in the same column (↕).

49

116

Twelve animals have birthdays in twelve different months. Which animal was born in which month?

- Lambie was born in a month which has a leap day.
- Rhinoceros has a birthday between Otter and Elephant.
- Walrus has more animals celebrating birthdays after her each year than before.
- Sloth's birthday is surrounded by Eagle and Mole.
- Eagle will have a birthday before Otter each year.
- Lion has a birthday three months before Squid.
- Polar Bear was born in the last month of the year.
- Mole will celebrate his birthday five months after Crab.
- Crab has the next birthday after Lambie.
- Otter has fewer people celebrating birthdays after him each year than before.
- Squid has a birthday eight months before Polar Bear.
- Elephant's birthday celebration is ten months after Lion's.

Can you draw lines to connect each animal to the month they were born in?

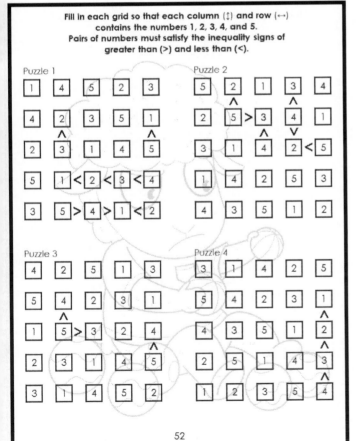

	Month		Month		Month
LION	January	LAMBIE	February	CRAB	March
SQUID	April	WALRUS	May	EAGLE	June
SLOTH	July	MOLE	August	OTTER	September
RHINOCEROS	October	ELEPHANT	November	POLAR BEAR	December

50

Fill in each grid so that each column (↕) and row (↔) contains the numbers 1, 2, 3, 4, and 5.
Boxes connected by a line mean the numbers are consecutive.
The absence of a line means numbers are not consecutive.

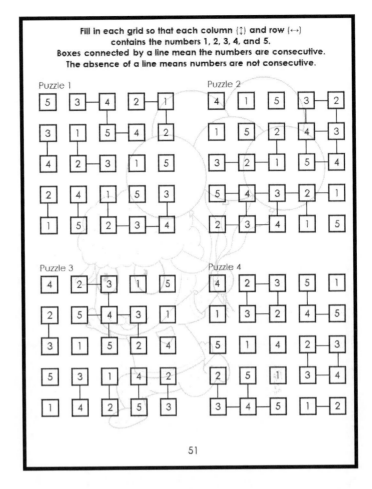

51

Fill in each grid so that each column (↕) and row (↔) contains the numbers 1, 2, 3, 4, and 5.
Pairs of numbers must satisfy the inequality signs of greater than (>) and less than (<).

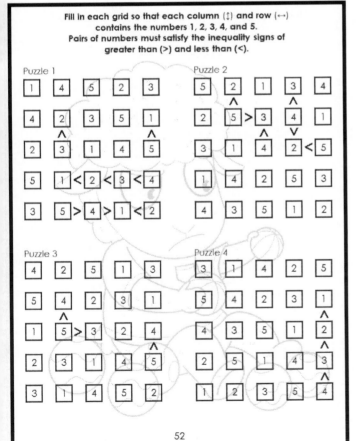

52

Can you connect each animal to their location?

- Leopard is next to Lambie, Giraffe, and Seal.
- Peacock is next to Spider and Owl.
- Fox is next to Mouse.
- Toad is next to Peacock, Turkey, Giraffe, and Mouse.
- Mouse is next to Toad, Elephant, and Owl.
- Spider is in the same row (↔) as Turkey and Lambie.
- One of the clues above is wrong.

SPIDER	TURKEY	FOX	LAMBIE
PEACOCK	TOAD	GIRAFFE	LEOPARD
OWL	MOUSE	ELEPHANT	SEAL

53

117

Connect the matching shapes without overlapping any lines or shapes.

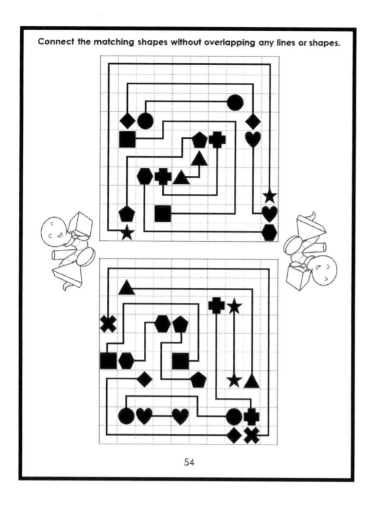

54

How long was everyone in the pool?

- Pool hours are 10:00am to 5:00pm.
- Alligator got in the pool when it opened and stayed in until noon.
- Beaver swam from 11:00am to 1:30pm with a 45-minute lunch break.
- Crab got in 15 minutes after Beaver and got out 30 minutes after Duck.
- Duck was in the pool twice as long as Alligator, and got out an hour before it closed.
- Lambie started swimming with Duck and got out with Salamander, but took three 15-minute breaks.
- Salamander swam for 30 minutes less than the next lowest animal and got out at 2:15pm.
- Platypus was at the pool from open until close, but only spent half her time swimming.
- Hippo started swimming with Salamander and got out an hour before Crab.

Can you fill out the gray boxes to show how long everybody spent in the pool and then order them from lowest total pool time to highest?

	Total Pool Time	Order		Total Pool Time	Order
Alligator	2 hours 0 minutes	4	Lambie	1 hours 30 minutes	2
Beaver	1 hours 45 minutes	3	Salamander	1 hours 0 minutes	1
Crab	5 Hours 15 minutes	8	Platypus	3 hours 30 minutes	6
Duck	4 hours 0 minutes	7	Hippo	2 hours 15 minutes	5

55

Who ate the last piece of cake?

Lambie was saving the last piece of cake for dessert tonight, but he just discovered it had been eaten! He asks his friends about it.

- Meerkat says, "Vulture ate it!"
- Camel says, "Meerkat is telling the truth!"
- Gorilla says, "If Meerkat is lying, Camel is lying."
- Vulture says, "It wasn't Camel."
- Platypus saw the whole thing and says, "Only one of those animals is telling the truth."

Can you help Lambie use the clues to figure out who ate the last piece of cake? Write your answer in the gray box below.

Camel ate the last piece of cake.
56

What is the three-digit combination for Lambie's bike lock?
Use these clues to help to figure it out.

9 8 2	6 5 4	4 1 6
One number is correct and in the correct position.	Two numbers are correct but placed incorrectly.	One number is correct but placed incorrectly.

7 8 5	7 3 8	3 4 9
One number is correct but placed incorrectly.	No numbers are correct.	One number is correct and in the correct position.

5 4 2
What is the combination?

57

If Meerkat was telling the truth, then Camel was telling the truth but since there is only one animal who was truthful, they both had to be lying. Therefore, Gorilla was telling the truth which means that Vulture was lying about it not being Camel.

Page 58

There is a race to the trophy! Each bird starts at the same time.
When they reach a shape, they fly the represented steps.

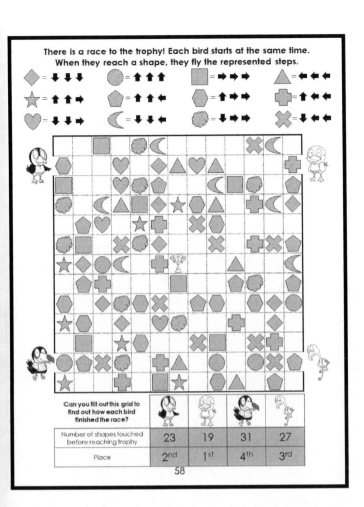

Can you fill out this grid to find out how each bird finished the race?				
Number of shapes touched before reaching trophy	23	19	31	27
Place	2nd	1st	4th	3rd

Page 59

Can you solve these brainteasers?
The answer may not be so obvious.

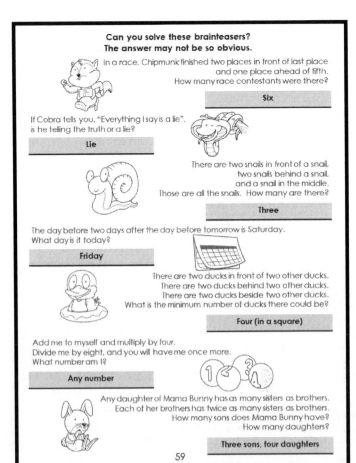

In a race, Chipmunk finished two places in front of last place and one place ahead of fifth. How many race contestants were there?

Six

If Cobra tells you, "Everything I say is a lie", is he telling the truth or a lie?

Lie

There are two snails in front of a snail, two snails behind a snail, and a snail in the middle. Those are all the snails. How many are there?

Three

The day before two days after the day before tomorrow is Saturday. What day is it today?

Friday

There are two ducks in front of two other ducks. There are two ducks behind two other ducks. There are two ducks beside two other ducks. What is the minimum number of ducks there could be?

Four (in a square)

Add me to myself and multiply by four. Divide me by eight, and you will have me once more. What number am I?

Any number

Any daughter of Mama Bunny has as many sisters as brothers. Each of her brothers has twice as many sisters as brothers. How many sons does Mama Bunny have? How many daughters?

Three sons, four daughters

Page 60

Draw a single non-intersecting line between dots to form a loop.
Numbers specify how many sides touch the loop. The first one is started.

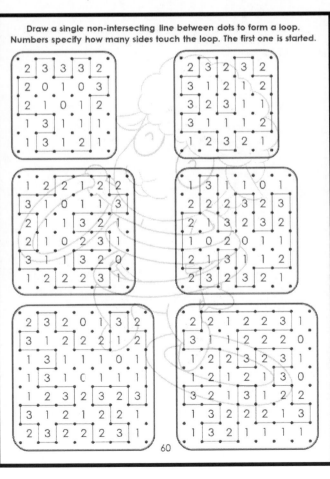

Page 61

Can you connect each animal to their location?

- Mouse is next to (4) and (7). Lambie is next to (6) and (8).
- The right-most column (↕) adds up to (16).
- The top-most row (↔) adds up to (19).
- All animals in the middle row (↔) are more than (5).
- Leopard is next to Giraffe and Fox.

MOUSE	SEAL	SPIDER	TOAD
GIRAFFE	LEOPARD	PEACOCK	TURKEY
OWL	FOX	ELEPHANT	LAMBIE

Numbers represent the amount of letters in the animal's name.

119

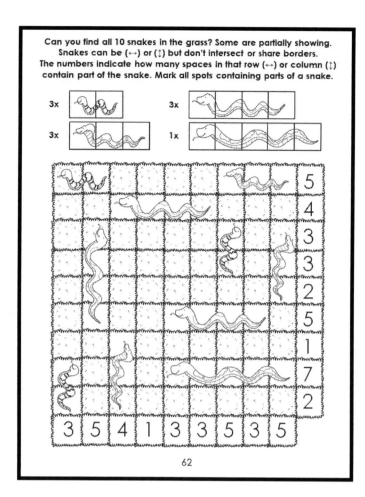

Can you find all 10 snakes in the grass? Some are partially showing. Snakes can be (↔) or (↕) but don't intersect or share borders. The numbers indicate how many spaces in that row (↔) or column (↕) contain part of the snake. Mark all spots containing parts of a snake.

Starting with the gray 'A', create a connected path that goes through the alphabet twice in order. You can connect letters horizontally (↔) and vertically (↕).

Sneaky Seagull is hungry and has stolen some food letters! Match each group of food words to the nest with the missing letter.

Trace the lines to find out which box contains each letter to reveal a secret message.

YOU ARE DOING GREAT!

Page 67

Color in every C, G, J, K, Q, and X.
The remaining letters show a hidden message.

Write the message below:

IF YOU FEEL OVERWHELMED ON A PUZZLE YOU START,
REMEMBER THE START IS THE HARDEST OF PARTS.

67

Page 68

Change one letter at a time moving from the top to bottom word.
Use the clues to help along your way.

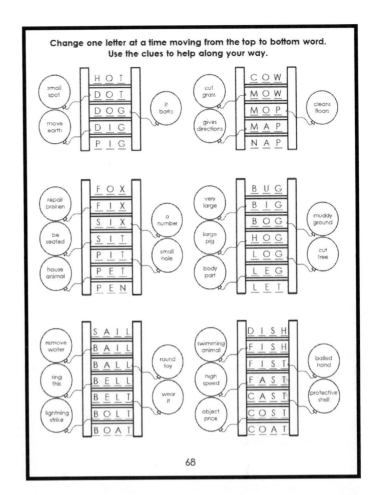

68

Page 69

Find the hidden words.
Words can go in these directions: ➡ ⬅ ⬆ ⬇ ⬈ ⬉ ⬊ ⬋

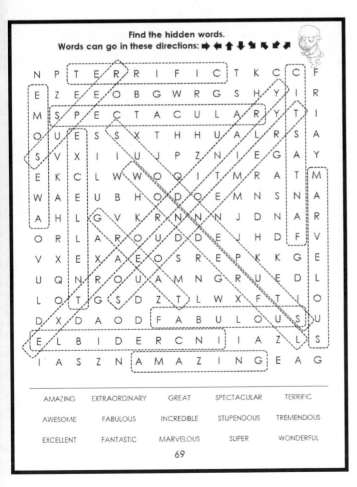

AMAZING	EXTRAORDINARY	GREAT	SPECTACULAR	TERRIFIC
AWESOME	FABULOUS	INCREDIBLE	STUPENDOUS	TREMENDOUS
EXCELLENT	FANTASTIC	MARVELOUS	SUPER	WONDERFUL

69

Page 70

Find the nine-letter animal names in each of these boxes.
Start at the gray box and connect to the next box
horizontally (↔), vertically (↕), or diagonally (⊠).

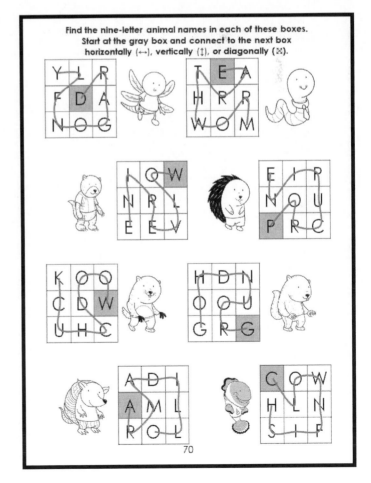

70

Page 71

Starting with the gray 'P', create a connected path that visits every square and spells each of the animals listed under the puzzle. You can connect letters horizontally (↔) or vertically (↕).

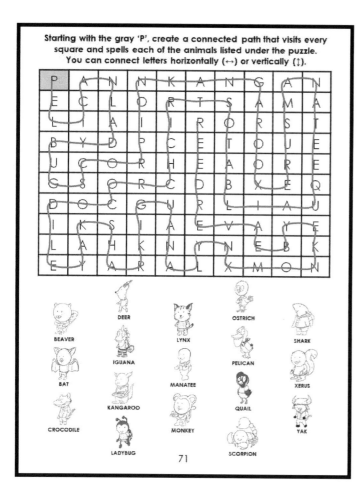

BEAVER DEER OSTRICH LYNX SHARK
IGUANA BAT PELICAN XERUS MANATEE
KANGAROO QUAIL CROCODILE MONKEY YAK
LADYBUG SCORPION

71

Page 72

For both sets of three baskets, pick a letter from the first basket, then second, then third. Using those three letters in order, can you write down at least ten words for both sets of baskets?

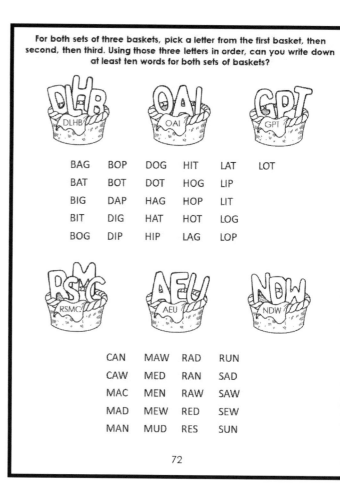

DLHB OAI GPT

BAG	BOP	DOG	HIT	LAT	LOT
BAT	BOT	DOT	HOG	LIP	
BIG	DAP	HAG	HOP	LIT	
BIT	DIG	HAT	HOT	LOG	
BOG	DIP	HIP	LAG	LOP	

RSMC AEU NDW

CAN	MAW	RAD	RUN
CAW	MED	RAN	SAD
MAC	MEN	RAW	SAW
MAD	MEW	RED	SEW
MAN	MUD	RES	SUN

72

Page 73

The grid below contains only animals. Numbers correspond to a particular letter. A few number-letter combinations are provided. Can you complete the rest? All letters A to Z are used at least once.

SHARK JACKAL WARTHOG OCTOPUS ALLIGATOR BUMBLEBEE DOLPHIN MOOSE BEAVER BADGER ROOSTER JAY

K B P F X G U I R D N A W
Z O T H Q E M C L V Y J S

A B C D E F G
H I J K L M N
O P Q R S T
U V W X Y Z

73

Page 74

Solve the clues to unlock the letters for the hidden phrase. You can also use a partially completed phrase to help solve the clues. Work the puzzle back and forth to find all the letters.

YOUR NEVER GIVE
UP ATTITUDE WILL
BRING SUCCESS TO
ALL YOU DO.

LAVA
27 16 12 42
molten rock

WEST
24 13 33 20
direction the sun sets

RUG
4 47 10
small floor covering

TOY
17 41 31
play with this

OVER
2 7 37 29
opposite of under

GLUE
32 44 3 23
sticky crafting object

SIT
38 30 18
___ in a chair

ICE
19 35 6
frozen water

LION
43 25 46 31
large cat with a mane

CUBE
36 14 28 8
three-dimensional square

SUN
39 34 5
provides daylight

OLD
49 26 22
not young

UP
21 15
opposite of down

DIRTY
48 11 9 40 45
needs to be cleaned

74

Page 75

Can you figure out the phrase for each of these word puzzles?
Consider how the words are written, the number of times,
their direction, and placement.

1 SHOES SHOES	2 LEAGUE	3 RECORD
4 GEGS GEGS / SGEG GGSE / SEGG ESGG / EGSG GESG	5 BOOK DUE	6 COLOR
7 RIGHT RIGHT THE CORNER RIGHT	8 TIME (reversed)	9 YGGIP RIDE

1 Pair of shoes	2 Little league	3 Broken record
4 Scrambled eggs	5 Book overdue	6 Color between the lines
7 Right around the corner	8 Halftime	9 Piggyback ride

75

Page 76

Drop letters in the appropriate square of each column (↕)
to make words and reveal a quote.
Two words in each puzzle have been done to help get you started.

O	N		T	H	A	T		J	O	U	R	N	E	Y
O	F		I	M	P	R	O	V	E	M	E	N	T	
I	T	S		F	U	N		T	O		F	I	N	D
Y	O	U		C	A	N		D	O		I	T		

T	H	E	R	E	S		A		L	E	S	S	O	N		I	N
T	H	E		L	O	S	I	N	G		Y	O	U	R	
R	E	S	P	O	N	S	E		I	S		Y	O	U	R
O	W	N		C	H	O	O	S	I	N	G	

76

Page 78

Use the picture below to answer the questions.

Circle the sheep which only appears one time.
Put squares around the sheep which appears most frequently.
Cross out the sheep which appear exactly five times.

How many unique kinds of sheep are there? 9

78

Page 79

Follow the path of hamsters to the finish!
You may move horizontally (↔) or vertically (↕) but must follow this order:

1 2 3 4

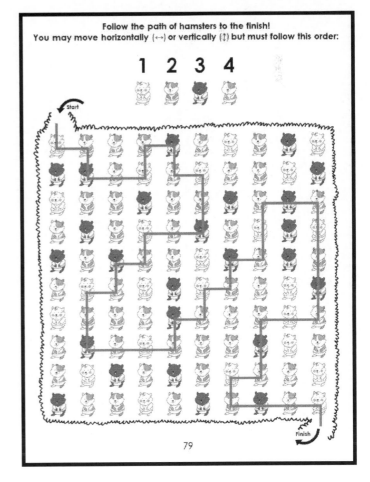

79

Connect the dots!

80

Count the objects hidden in the drawing.

| 9 | 8 | 3 | 4 | 6 |

81

Circle the two identical drawings.

82

Find and circle the hidden four-leaf clover.
There is only one!

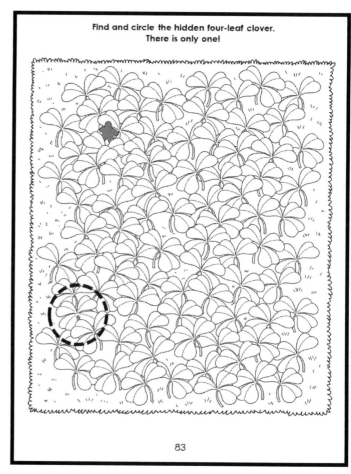

83

Fill in the triangles to reveal a picture!

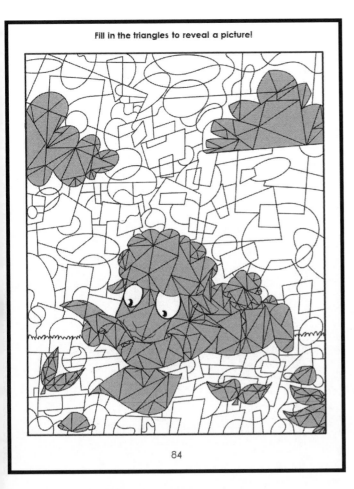

84

For the grids on the left, find and outline the clusters shown to the right.

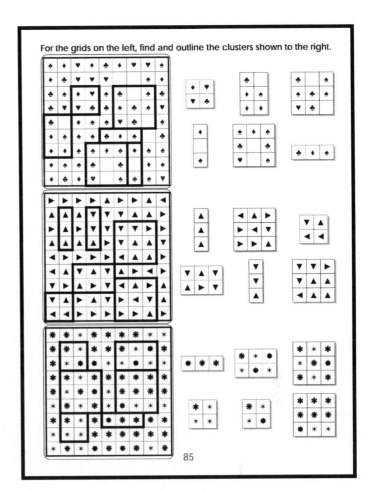

85

Fit the provided numbers into the grid.
A few answers have been filled in to help you get started.

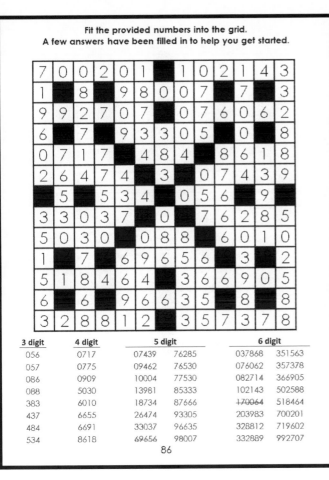

3 digit	4 digit	5 digit		6 digit	
056	0717	07439	76285	037868	351563
057	0775	09462	76530	076062	357378
086	0909	10004	77530	082714	366905
088	5030	13981	85333	102143	502588
383	6010	18734	87666	170064	518464
437	6655	26474	93305	203983	700201
484	6691	33037	96635	328812	719602
534	8618	69656	98007	332889	992707

86

Can you navigate the maze?

87

125

Reveal the hidden picture by coloring in squares in the correct location. The coordinates show where each piece fits into the grid.

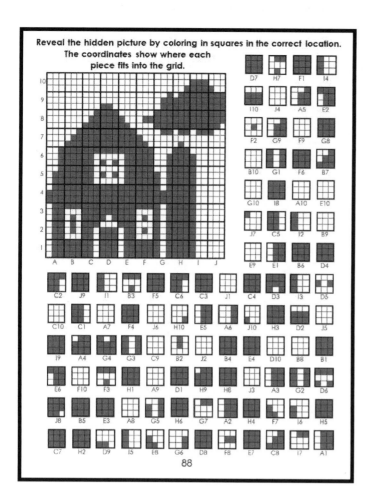

Hidden pictures!

Can you find?

88

89

Can you find and circle 16 differences between these pictures?

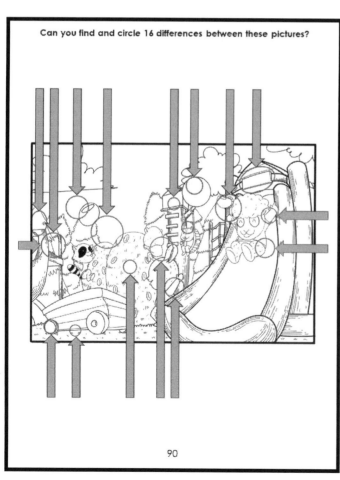

90

126

Certificate of
ACHIEVEMENT

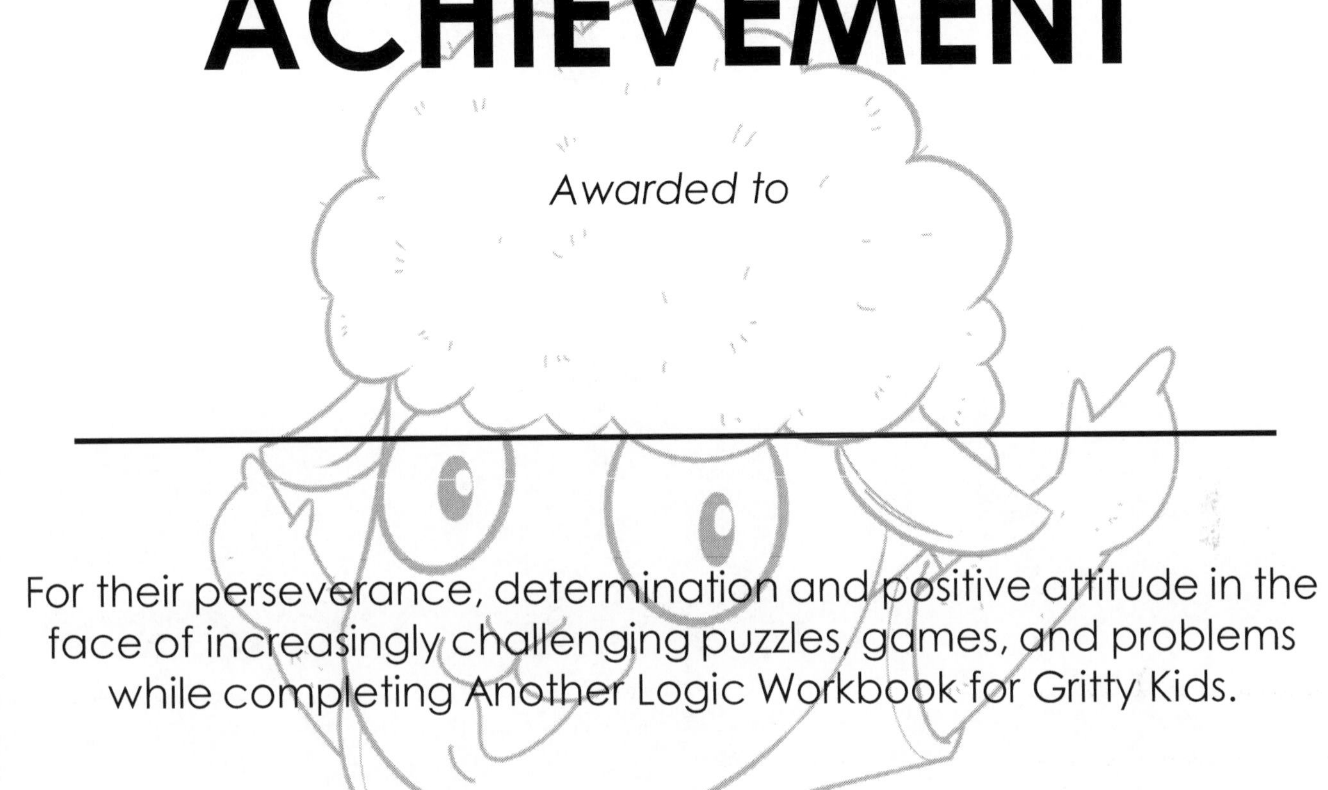

Awarded to

_____

For their perseverance, determination and positive attitude in the face of increasingly challenging puzzles, games, and problems while completing Another Logic Workbook for Gritty Kids.

This _____ day of _____ in the year of _____

Signed _____

ANOTHER
LOGIC WORKBOOK FOR
GRITTY
KIDS

THE GRITTY KIDS SERIES

Fostering grit, growth, and perseverance in children through games and stories.

for ages 3-8

for ages 6-10

for ages 8-12

for ages 3-6

for ages 5+

HIDDEN MEEPLE ANSWER!

page 83

To my parents,
For the countless times you've pushed me to be better.
For the love and support you've always provided.
For the obstacles you removed that I never even saw.
For the head starts you gave me.
For your guidance and wisdom.
I've never wanted. And for that I'm incredibly blessed.
-DA

To Him, to my family and friends,
I'm truly honored and glad for all the courage and motivation, all the support and comfort,
and all the time, trust and understanding that you all have given to me.
Another milestone for another great step yet ahead.
-AY

The following pages are intentionally blank to allow
space to further explore puzzles or play additional games.

Text © 2022 by Dan Allbaugh
Illustrations © 2022 by Anil Yap
ISBN: 978-1-7357708-5-7

Green Meeple Books

greenmeeplebooks.com

ANOTHER
LOGIC WORKBOOK FOR

GRITTY
KIDS
additional workspace

Made in the USA
Middletown, DE
08 February 2023

24309936R00082